W9-AMW-626

Stop Caretaking the Borderline
or Narcissist

Stop Caretaking the Borderline or Narcissist

How to End the Drama and Get On with Life

Margalis Fjelstad

ROWMAN & LITTLEFIELD PUBLISHERS, INC.
Lanham • Boulder • New York • London

Published by Rowman & Littlefield
A wholly owned subsidiary of The Rowman & Littlefield Publishing Group, Inc.
4501 Forbes Boulevard, Suite 200, Lanham, Maryland 20706
www.rowman.com

16 Carlisle Street, London W1D 3BT, United Kingdom

Copyright © 2013 by Rowman & Littlefield Publishers, Inc.
First paperback edition 2014

All rights reserved. No part of this book may be reproduced in any form or by any electronic or mechanical means, including information storage and retrieval systems, without written permission from the publisher, except by a reviewer who may quote passages in a review.

British Library Cataloguing in Publication Information Available

Library of Congress Cataloging-in-Publication Data

The hardback edition of this book was previously catalogued by the Library of Congress as follows:

Fjelstad, Margalis, 1945–
Stop caretaking the borderline or narcissist : how to end the drama and get on with life / Margalis Fjelstad.
p. cm.
Includes bibliographical references and index.
1. Narcissism. 2. Narcissists—Family relationships. 3. Enabling (Psychology) 4. Codependency. I. Title.
BF575.N35F54 2013
155.2'32—dc23
2012040275

ISBN 978-1-4422-2018-8 (cloth : alk. paper)
ISBN 978-1-4422-3832-9 (pbk. : alk. paper)
ISBN 978-1-4422-2019-5 (electronic)

∞ The paper used in this publication meets the minimum requirements of American National Standard for Information Sciences Permanence of Paper for Printed Library Materials, ANSI/NISO Z39.48-1992.

Printed in the United States of America

This above all—to thine ownself be true; And it must follow, as the night the day, Thou canst not then be false to any man. —William Shakespeare, *Hamlet*

Contents

I

Understanding the Caretaker Role

INTRODUCTION: HOW CAN YOU TELL IF YOU'RE A CARETAKER?

Is your stomach in knots much of the time? Do have headaches or backaches and feel tense too much of the time around your partner? And do these feelings alternate with a sense of total bliss and relaxation when your partner is "in a good mood"? Do you feel like you're living with two different people, one who is loving and attentive and one who is mean, angry, critical, and attacking at other times? Do you wish the person you married was the person who is there with you all of the time?

Do you feel responsible to make your life together work by being perfect, always trying to be there to meet your partner's needs and making amends even when you're not sure what you did? Do you try to cheer her up, but even when things are going really well she gets depressed? Do you try to soothe him when he is angry and storms off in the middle of a family gathering? Do you even feel responsible when she feels suicidal?

Does it come second nature to you to think you did something wrong when someone else is upset? Do you hate conflict? Are you competent and effective at work and seem to get along with almost everyone, yet at home your spouse accuses you of being selfish, uncaring, hurtful, and thoughtless?

Do you take these accusations from your loved one time after time, trying harder and harder to make things right and then, when you are finally frustrated, explode, feel guilty, and blame yourself for not being able to please your partner? When you were growing up, did you have a family member, mother, father, sibling, or grandparent who acted like your partner acts today?

Do you just wish for a peaceful, calm life that is predictable, supportive, friendly, and easygoing? Do you feel taken advantage of when you are trying hard to do a good job and your partner slacks off and yet gets all the praise and attention? Do you feel a sense of guilt, foreboding, and confusion when you think about your life? Do you often feel tired, overwhelmed, and alone in your relationship? Have you tried numerous times to work on your relationship with your partner but nothing ever seems to change?

If these descriptions are a picture of your life, if you feel like you are in a "crazy-making" relationship, if you feel you are becoming more depressed and anxious rather than the easygoing, calm person you were before this relationship, it is very likely that you are a Caretaker for a borderline/narcissist person.

How did you get to this place? More important, how can you get out of this place? That's what this book is all about.

No, you are not crazy. But you are in a crazy-making relationship. If your life seems calm, positive, and moving forward outside of this relationship but this relationship feels like the description above, you are probably involved with a borderline or narcissistic person. This book will be describing the symptoms of the borderline and narcissism disorders as well as how you got hooked into being a Caretaker. We will look at why you got into and continue to stay in this relationship, your role in making the relationship work, and the things you can do to change it.

Your focus since you became involved with the borderline/narcissist has been on him or her. You may have found yourself thinking more about your partner's thoughts, feelings, needs, wants, and behaviors than you think about your own. You may have the mistaken idea that this is normal in relationships, but it isn't. Your increasing depression, anxiety, tension, and confusion aren't normal either. In fact, you may have completely lost your sense of what is normal.

This book is about getting back to a normal life, a healthy life, your life. It's about learning to defocus from the borderline/narcissist's dramas, over-the-top emotionality, and push/pull, love/hate interactions and going back to creating a peaceful, enjoyable, low-key life that is healthy, positive, and relaxing.

Being in a relationship with a borderline/narcissist can be intoxicating, full of spontaneity, exciting, and thrilling. You may feel deeply needed and super important to him or her. At the same time, this life is all about them and none about you. You may have even lost sight of who you are and what you want, and your own interests, feelings, and needs. You may have even lost friends and family connections because of the borderline/narcissist.

A healthy relationship is one that nurtures and reflects both partners. It fulfills the needs of both people—and it attends to the goals and interests and desires of both people. It is not always on high alert. Decisions in healthy relationships are made calmly after a discussion of both people's needs and wants and people follow through with what they say they are going to do. A healthy relationship gives you energy, helps you feel relaxed, and makes you feel wanted and comfortable just the way you already are.

I'll leave it to you to decide if this book is what you are looking for. If you feel you have lost yourself, there is something crazy about your relationship, or you are slowly wearing down into a pessimistic, anxious, and hopeless person, then you may be a Caretaker in relationship with a borderline/narcissist. Start out by taking the Caretaker Test in the appendix and then read about how these relationships function. If this fits for you; if you want to learn to have loving, healthy relationships; and if you want to take charge of your own life and create the happiness you would like to have, then this book can point the way.

Chapter One

Is My Partner Really a Borderline or Narcissist?

WHAT IS A PERSONALITY DISORDER?

Personality is considered to be the pattern of behaviors, motivations, thoughts, ways of speaking, sense of self, individual quirkiness, and so on that is unique to a specific person. We "know" a person by his or her personality. We think of personality as a pretty stable (though not totally unchanging) way that a person thinks, feels, and behaves. It is not clearly measurable, but neither is the amount of pain a person is feeling, and it can't be pinpointed in a certain part of the brain. Personality seems to be the sum total of our genetic and learned experiences and the way we put millions of pieces of experience together to form a whole sense of self. Typically, we expect ourselves and our friends and family to maintain pretty much the same personalities over our lifetime, and we usually do.

There is an orderly way of learning to be a person. As our brains develop and we interact with our parents and friends, we develop stable ways of defining ourselves and our relationships. As we grow to adulthood, we learn the rules of social interaction. We move from dependency to increasing autonomy. We learn who we are in relation to others, and we develop an understanding of what to expect in our dealings with other people. We develop a sense of esteem, that is, caring, concern, and value for ourselves. We learn that we can pretty much count on being basically the same person with the same behaviors and social abilities from day to day. We also learn to count on others in the same way.

However, something seems to go amiss in this orderly development for people who become disabled with borderline personality disorder (BPD) and narcissistic personality disorder (NPD). Because of a biological sensitivity to emotional stress, some people do not process information about the world in such an orderly fashion. They tend to have a "highly sensitive" emotional system that reacts instantaneously and intensely to their experiences. They do not adjust to change very well or very quickly. They do not respond to soothing and nurturing as easily as other children. [1]

If these "highly sensitive" children experience traumatic or abandoning experiences or have nonresponsive or invalidating parenting, they are very susceptible to failing to develop a fully matured, adult personality. [2] Therapists since Freud have observed that trauma, abandonment, or being poorly nurtured can result in the child's personality development being impaired and stunted at the stage of development where the loss or trauma occurred. Recent research also has noted that genetic vulnerabilities and even prenatal injury or infection may also be influencing factors. Since personality is a constant building-up process of adding more and more awareness and skills to a base, those children with a weakened or incomplete base will just not fully learn all that they need to as they grow up. And what they learn may be distorted by their upsetting experiences. [3]

People with BPD and NPD seem to get "stuck" or impaired at fairly early levels of emotional development, usually around 18 to 24 months of age. As adults, they have the mental content, vocabulary, and experiences of adults; however, their ability to process complex, personal, intimate relationships has not developed beyond those early childhood levels. Developmental psychologists point out that there are "optimal" times when learning patterns of human interaction are much easier and that after the optimal time it may be extremely difficult or impossible to fully learn new ways of thinking and interacting.

Specific patterns of personality impairment in person-to-person functioning have been identified by therapists and researchers. The two patterns of impairment that we are looking at in this book are BPD and NPD. These two disorders share many similarities and some obvious differences. They are serious mental illnesses, and they have a profound impact on family members as well.

How does a person with BPD or NPD affect their children, spouse, and family? How does the role of Caretaker develop in response to a family member having a personality disorder? Because people with BPD and NPD make such a profound impact on their family members, the family itself cannot keep functioning without someone taking the Caretaker role. How does the Caretaker role keep healthy family members from reaching their own full emotional development and satisfaction? How can the Caretaker remove him- or herself from this role and learn to create a healthier and more satisfactory life? These are the questions we will look at throughout this book.

Let's look first at the patterns of BPD and NPD, keeping in mind that these patterns are variable and unique to each person. It is probably best to think of people with these disorders being on a continuum from some impairment in a few areas to severe impairment in most or all areas. Naturally, your own family member may be anywhere on the continuum, and it is good to keep in mind that an individual may act more impaired when under severe emotional stress and seem less impaired when there is very little change, conflict, or responsibility to deal with.

BORDERLINE PERSONALITY DISORDER (BPD)

The clinical term "borderline personality disorder" came into use to describe ongoing, long-lasting dysfunctional behaviors in people who did not have a full-blown psychosis, such as schizophrenia, but who also were significantly more dysfunctional than people with problems of anxiety and depression. BPD is described by the *Diagnostic and Statistical Manual of Mental Disorders* (4th ed.) (*DSM-IV*) as a "pervasive pattern of instability of interpersonal relationships, self-image and affects or moods, and marked impulsivity, beginning by early adulthood and present in a variety of contexts," including at least five of the following:[4]

1. *Frantic efforts to avoid real or imagined abandonment.* Persons with BPD may not be willing or able to do much of anything alone. The borderline person, or BP, can become frantic over events such as having lunch alone or having to be at home alone at night. BPs may drink, call loved ones dozens of times an hour, go out and pick up a stranger for sex, have crying fits, or cut themselves to avoid being alone. The more dramatic, intense, and self-destructive the BP's behaviors, the more dysfunctional the person usually is.

2. *A pattern of unstable and intense interpersonal relationships.* This refers to the pattern of the BP going from intense love and adoration to intense hate, rage, and anger over and over in love relationships. BPs are known for being happy one minute and threatening divorce a few minutes later. They break up with loved ones, only to get back together and break up over and over.

3. *Unstable self-image or sense of self.* The BP may not believe that he or she exists in the mind of others unless the other person is in direct contact and giving direct feedback to the BP. The BP can receive a loving comment and in the same conversation state that she believes she is not loved or even thought well of by the other person. The BP alternately sees himself as all good or all bad, superior or inferior,

caring or hateful. The BP finds it hard to hold in mind different feelings and different qualities of personality together at the same time.

4. *Impulsivity.* Because the BP has strong, wildly fluctuating emotions that are extremely intense, he or she often acts impulsively and may respond suddenly with extremely negative or extremely positive emotions. He may throw things, walk out of an anniversary dinner, shout profanities in public, or send dozens of red roses or propose to a new love he's just met a few hours earlier. Often the BP responds quite differently to the same situation at different times. This makes it very hard to predict how a BP may act in any given moment.

5. *Recurrent suicidal behavior, gestures, or threats of self-mutilation.* The BP's emotional reactions to disappointment, loss, fear, anxiety, or abandonment can be extreme. She can believe that the current feeling will, literally, *never* go away, so suicide can seem to be the only answer. Cutting or burning herself with cigarettes may be used by the BP to decrease her awareness of her emotional pain by focusing on a concrete physical pain.

6. *Mood instability, reactivity, depression, anxiety, rage, and despair.* This is a hallmark of BPD. The BP is extremely vulnerable to falling into negative moods in an instant and is usually very fast to change moods, sometimes within seconds or minutes, and these emotions can fluctuate quickly back and forth. These emotions are often extremely strong, and the BP is at a loss as to how to handle them alone.

7. *Chronic feelings of emptiness.* The BP may feel invisible and often does not believe that anyone remembers her when she is not in that person's presence. She may expect others to not think about her when she is gone but at the same time may be enraged by not having her needs anticipated. She may have no sense of who she is, what she wants in life, or what her skills, values, or beliefs are, but she may also expect a loved one to know these things for her.

8. *Inappropriate intense anger or difficulty controlling anger.* The intensity of the BP's anger can be shocking to others around him. The BP may act physically abusive, striking out by hitting, throwing things, screaming, threatening harm, or, in extreme cases, killing the loved one. He can also act in emotionally abusive ways through blaming, put-downs, impossible demands, and ultimatums. The BP cannot seem to let go of such intense anger even with the attention of a loved one. If the BP feels an emotion, whatever it is, that feeling is absolutely true to the BP and cannot be changed by logic. Because the BP cannot figure out how the emotion came about, he or she usually blames someone else for causing the feeling.

9. *Transient, stress-related paranoid ideas or severe dissociative symptoms.* This is the most confusing symptom demonstrated by the BP.

The BP can instantaneously change from seeing a loved one as precious and supportive person to seeing the same loved one as a threatening enemy. As a result, the BP can say things and act toward her spouse and child in ways that she would do only to her worst, most hated enemy. In addition, the BP typically forgets what he said and did a few hours or a day later, and he almost never understands the emotional impact of his outburst on his loved ones. While the hurtful words and actions still sting in the other person, the BP sees no reason to apologize or even discuss what happened because as far as the BP is concerned, it never even happened or is "all in the past."

Another way to get an even clearer picture of borderline behaviors is to look at the five areas of unstable, erratic, dysfunctional, and unpredictable behaviors that have been identified by Marsha Linehan in people with BPD. The following examples of these daily behaviors, thoughts, and feelings of the BP might seem clearer than the therapeutic descriptions by the *DSM-IV*.

Emotional Instability

- Intense emotional neediness, which may be covered up by a facade of independence.
- Sudden emotional outbursts of rage and despair that seem random.
- Belief that the emotions of the moment are totally accurate and will last forever.
- Inaccurate memory of emotional events, even changing the meaning of the events after the fact.
- Seeing their emotions as being *caused* by others or by events outside themselves, with no belief that they have any sort of control over their own emotions.
- Believing that the only way to change how they feel is to get other people or events to change.
- Ongoing, intense anxiety and fear.

Thought Instability

- All-or-nothing thinking (e.g., loving you intensely and just as quickly reversing to hating you or thinking that they are a total failure or, conversely, immensely superior).
- Intense belief in their own perceptions despite facts to the contrary.
- Their interpretation of events is the only truth.
- Constantly searching for the "hidden meaning" (always negative) in conversations and events.
- Cannot be persuaded by fact or logic.

- Do not see the effect of their own behavior on others.
- Deny the perceptions of others.
- Accuse others of saying and doing things they didn't say or do.
- Deny (even forget) negative or positive events from the past that conflict with current feelings.

Behavioral Instability

- Impulsive behavior (e.g., sexual acting out, reckless behavior, gambling, going into dangerous situations with little awareness, or shoplifting).
- Physically, sexually, or emotionally abusive to others.
- May cut, burn, or mutilate themselves.
- Often have addictions to alcohol, prescription or street drugs (especially for pain relief or for sleep), spending money, eating disorders, or other compulsive behaviors.
- Create crises and chaos continuously.
- Often quickly go to suicidal thoughts when disappointed or disagreed with.

Instability of a Sense of Self

- Intense fear or paranoia about being rejected, even to the extent that they need to be approved of by people they don't like.
- Often change their persona, opinions, or beliefs, depending on who they are with.
- Lack of a consistent sense of who they are or may have a overly rigid picture of the self.
- Often present a facade. May be fearful of being seen for "who I really am." Automatically assuming that they will be rejected or criticized.
- May never have formed any real beliefs, opinions, or interests of their own.
- Act inappropriately or outrageously to get attention.
- Have difficulty adjusting to changes in the looks of loved ones (e.g., new mustache, haircut, or new style of dress).
- Out of sight, out of mind. Difficulty realizing that they or others exist when not together.
- Simultaneously see themselves as both inferior and superior to others.

Relationship Instability

- Instantly fall in love or instantly end a relationship with no logical explanation.

- Hostile, devaluing verbal attacks on loved ones while being charming and pleasant to strangers.
- Overidealization of others (e.g., difficulty allowing others to be less than perfect, be vulnerable, or make mistakes).
- Have trouble being alone even for short periods of time yet also push people away by picking fights.
- Blaming, accusing, and attacking loved ones for small, even trivial mistakes or accidents.
- May try to avoid anticipated rejection by rejecting the other person first.
- Difficulty feeling loved if the other person is not around.
- Highly controlling and demanding of others.
- Unwilling to recognize and respect the limits of others.
- Demand rights, commitments, and behaviors from others that they are not willing or able to reciprocate.

Listen as Merrilee describes her mother's borderline behaviors: "My mother would be in the middle of making dinner and begin a shouting match with my father about how he never really loved her like her old boyfriend in high school because he had just told her he had some reports to work on after dinner. She would yell and slam pots around and then stomp out of the kitchen, and that was the end of dinner. Sometimes she would go to bed and we wouldn't see her again for two days. Other times she would put on her coat and leave the house. Sometimes she came back late, and sometimes my dad would have to go find her. Once she got drunk and took a plane to St. Louis. Dad went and got her. The day after she came home, she acted like nothing had ever happened, and she never referred to the incident again."

DIFFICULTY IDENTIFYING BPD

BPD is difficult to identify because many of the above behaviors are ones that anyone could have on occasion, especially under stress. For the BP, however, it is more a difference of intensity, frequency, and choice. In the BP, these behaviors can occur several times a week, several times a day, or even several times an hour. They can be shockingly sudden and intense, and they don't seem to be entirely under the control of the BP. Situations that are not particularly stressful for an emotionally healthy person can be overwhelming to the BP. The BP's upset often seems to come "out of the blue."

It is also important to remember that no two BPs act completely alike. It is the unique events of each person's life that make up the *content* of the fears and distorted thinking in the BP. In addition, it can be hard to clearly identify BPD because the BP may use alcohol, prescription medication, and/or illegal drugs or have another mental illness (e.g., bipolar disorder, attention deficit disorder, or obsessive-compulsive disorder) that can cause confusion because of some similar symptoms and behaviors.

More and more, the cause of BPD is being seen as having a genetic or biological vulnerability that is brought out when certain high-stress parenting and family environments are present.[5] The person with fully diagnosable BPD has a long, hard road to better health. The BP usually does not make significant changes without medication and years, perhaps decades, of intensive therapy. It is important for people who are Caretakers to recognize that BPD is an illness with lifelong symptoms and ramifications.

The diagnosis of BPD by a therapist or doctor doesn't usually occur until the person has started acting inappropriately in public, has gotten into trouble with the law, or has attempted suicide or cutting. Behaviors must be extreme and pervasive, and the person is usually in need of a psychiatric inpatient program before the disorder comes to the notice of people outside the family. In fact, very few of the people with these behaviorial patterns ever become clinically diagnosed as BPD, but often they will be treated for one or more of their individual symptoms, such as anxiety, depression, alcoholism, chronic job conflicts, domestic violence, rage, and so on.

The BP's behavior can be improved by quitting drugs or alcohol, getting on medication, learning "appropriate" behaviors, or lowering stress, but it does not cure the disorder. BPD is typically considered a lifelong problem in emotional dysfunction, and these extremely erratic behaviors appear over and over under stress even while on medication or in therapy.

NARCISSISTIC PERSONALITY DISORDER (NPD)

You may be more familiar with the personality pattern of narcissism. Narcissism has come into the popular vocabulary, but only part of the personality behavior pattern is usually observed. The flamboyant, selfish behaviors are the ones most people see and identify as narcissistic. The *DSM-IV* describes the person with NPD as having the following:

An increased sense of importance
Preoccupations with fantasies of success, wealth, beauty, and talent
A strong sense of being unique and special
A sense of entitlement to being treated better than others
Exploitation of others
Unwilling or unable to notice or understand other's feelings
Envy and arrogance

These behaviors are pretty well known. The part of the pattern that is usually not known by most people is the hidden, self-loathing, fear of rejection, and inner anxiety of the NP. Narcissists are people with two different self-esteems. There is a false sense of self (i.e., a pretend self that is extremely positive and desirable) and the hidden real self underneath the facade that is fearful and anxious.[6]

People with either BPD or NPD have core feelings of low self-esteem and worthlessness (even self-hatred), emotional fear, vulnerability, and loneliness. However, narcissists usually hide these negative feelings from others by creating a more attractive and charming false self that they present to the world. The NP acts more sociable, likable, and quite often charismatic in public and acts out his or her emotionally explosive, volatile, and hostile feelings in the privacy of the family, especially when under pressure. Because NPs seem to have more control over their behavior and emotional responses, they are more often described as having an underlying feeling of maliciousness and calculation in their attacks on others, whereas the borderline seems to be automatically reacting to intense, inner impulses without much conscious control or direction.

DIAGNOSING NPD

The diagnosis of NPD is also rarely given by professionals, but it is often used by the general population to refer to publicity-seeking actors, "show-offs," people who seem self-important, and those who act consistently selfish. Fewer people with NPD enter therapy than other groups because they usually function very well in the world using their false self and have a great loathing to being seen as inadequate, crazy, inferior, or dependent. In other words, NPs feel a strong need to protect their real, inner feelings from rejection and derision. As long as they can maintain a false self, NPs are rarely willing to explore the inner pain and fear that they carry. Usually, the NP enters therapy when his or her negative inner sense of self rises to the surface because of a major loss, humiliation, disappointment, debilitating accident, or being sent by a concerned employer.

THE NEGATIVE DIAGNOSES

Other significant reasons that people are not often officially diagnosed with BPD or NPD include the following:

1. The terms "borderline" and "narcissist" are often used casually by professionals and the public in derogatory ways.
2. Patients may react with anger and hostility when given either diagnosis.
3. Insurance companies consider these disorders as "incurable" and often do not pay therapists for a patient's treatment.

4. Once labeled with BPD or NPD, the person may lose all hope of improving in therapy and give up.
5. Very few therapists or physicians are trained or have experience in identifying and treating these disorders.

Indeed, the terms "borderline" or "narcissist" are too often used as negative put-downs rather than as helpful information.

HOW BORDERLINES AND NARCISSISTS ARE ALIKE AND DIFFERENT

Narcissists and borderlines present themselves to the world in opposite ways, as the light and the dark, the charming and the hostile, or the positive and the negative of each other. They appear rather like a pair of opposites on the outside. The borderline acts emotionally more negative, less social, less predictable, and more dependent. The narcissist acts more friendly, outgoing, outrageously optimistic, fantastically competent, and in control. Despite the differences in these two external personality patterns, borderlines and narcissists share a similar internal sense of low self-esteem, fear, anxiety, paranoia, and deep emotional pain from a sense of "not feeling good enough." Both will also go to extremes to protect their emotional vulnerability. Most important, both use many of the same *defense mechanisms*: blaming, projection, devaluing, idealization, splitting, denial, distortion, rationalization, and passive-aggressiveness. Narcissists also use omnipotence, whereas borderlines will use acting out. Sometimes these defense mechanisms can reach delusional or psychotic levels.

Because of these internal emotional similarities and their similar use of defense mechanisms in interpersonal and intimate relationships, close family members who deal with the BP or NP will see many similar behaviors. The fears and needs of both are very much alike. Both need a Caretaker to provide extensive validation, to let them have control over the relationship, to give them an unending amount of attention, and to reassure them that they and the Caretaker have the same thoughts, feelings, and beliefs.

Throughout this book, I will use the initials BP/NP when referring to behaviors that are similar for both borderlines and narcissists. The use of BP will refer only to borderline persons and NP to narcissist persons when their behaviors are typically different.

CARETAKER PERSONALITY

People who become Caretakers for a BP/NP also seem to have a certain set of personality traits. These traits do not constitute a "personality disorder." In fact, they can be highly valued and useful to relationships and families, at work, and socially, especially when they are at moderate levels. They include a desire to do a good job, enjoyment in pleasing others, a desire to care for others, peacemaking, a gentle and mild temperament, and calm and reasonable behaviors. These traits can be the hallmark of someone who is easy to get along with, caring of others, and a good worker, spouse, and parent.

But when you use these behaviors as a means of counteracting the extreme behaviors of the BP/NP, they can morph into more toxic forms and become perfectionism, a need to please, overcompliance, extreme guilt, anxiety, overconcern, avoidance of conflict, fear of anger, low self-esteem, and passivity. At that point, these traits become detrimental to the mental, emotional, and physical health of the person and become Caretaker behaviors.

This book will look at how someone moves from being a caring person to being a Caretaker and the effects of that role. We will look at factors that contribute to these more extreme reactions, how they impact your life as a Caretaker, how Caretakers are set up for failure, how to get out of the Caretaker role, and how to become that loving, caring person you want to be.

FURTHER NOTE

Even though I have gone into some detail about specific symptoms for BPD and NPD, I do so to give you as clear a picture of the intensity, amazing range, and severity of these behaviors. Seeing these behaviors in your loved one is confusing, upsetting, crazy-making, and intolerable. You may see them in your spouse or parent, an adult child, a coworker, or a friend. There may be more than one BP/NP in your life.

Because only a professional can reliably diagnose someone with BPD or NPD, we will look at these patterns of symptoms in emotions, behaviors, thoughts, and relationships as the basis for understanding the debilitating interactions you have learned to cope with in these toxic relationships in your life. As a Caretaker, it is important that you learn to identify when you are dealing with someone who has these behaviors because they trigger your unhealthy response behaviors. You can gain control over your responses only when you can see the patterns of interaction that you are playing into. By knowing consciously what kind of interactions you are involved in, you can make better choices about when to use your own energy for caring for others and when to focus on caring for yourself instead. So don't get too stuck on the labels; rather, look at the actual behaviors, emotional reactions, and intensity levels described in this chapter to understand who and what you are dealing with.

Before moving on, take the Caretaker Test in this book's appendix. This will help you identify what caretaking behaviors you are using.

Chapter Two

Why the Borderline/Narcissist Needs a Caretaker

How do families become dominated by a BP/NP, and how do these families differ from "normal" families? In a normal family, the needs and wants of all the members are pretty well balanced. The parents care for the children and each other, and the children learn to be helpful, according to their ability.[1] However, in the NP/BP family, the needs and wants of the BP/NP significantly dominate the time, money, and energy of the entire family. The spouse of the BP/NP spends most of his or her time taking care of the BP/NP, and the children are expected to act like adults by taking care of themselves as well as doing what they can to appease the BP/NP. This results in reversed roles with parents acting childish and children being overly responsible. A lot of gaps in learning and a lot of mislearning about relationships occur as well.[2]

LIVING WITH THE BORDERLINE/NARCISSIST PERSON

If you live with a BP/NP, you know how he or she "really" acts day to day. The family environment is where the BP/NP acts out emotional fears, need for control, and anxiety about being too close or too distant. As the spouse and/or child of a BP/NP, it is you who finds yourself alone dealing with these manipulative, hurtful, bizarre, and infuriating behaviors. The BP/NP can often pull it together for years to get through daily work situations, perhaps lying to their doctors and friends to keep their controlling and emotionally volatile behavior hidden. Too often, you and other family members collude with the BP/NP in this cover-up, even when the BP/NP may be doing illegal behaviors, such as stealing your identity, forging prescriptions, draining your bank account, or being physically abusive. This collusion to make the BP/NP and the family look normal and function as a unit is the job of the Caretaker.

HOW THE BORDERLINE/NARCISSIST FUNCTIONS
IN RELATIONSHIPS

The BP/NP has much more intense reactions to all of their feelings than normal individuals. These negative feelings are so upsetting that they try to push them away by projecting them onto someone else, especially someone who is emotionally and intimately close, such as a child or a spouse. The BP/NP has a desperate *need* to have someone in his or her life to carry these overwhelming negative feelings, someone to accuse of causing the internal pain, someone to hate so as not to hate the self. This internal self-hatred is the real source of the BP/NP's pain and anguish. BP/NPs also need someone to rescue them from these overwhelming feelings, to ease and soothe their fears, and to make life feel safe and less overwhelming. The Caretakers in the family are expected to take care of these feelings for the BP/NP.

The BP/NP has a great many fears. BP/NPs are deeply afraid of being alone, being abandoned, being needy, being invisible, and being unloved. They struggle with a fear of emotionally dying or ceasing to exist if they don't get these fears soothed by someone else. BP/NPs have been known to pull people who are strangers into immediate closeness in order to transform the pain of being alone into the euphoria of intense "love," immediately believing that this is "the one" who will truly be all-loving and all-nurturing, someone with whom the BP/NP can fully immerse him- or herself.

At the same time, BP/NPs are also afraid of being close to anyone. They are afraid of being absorbed into someone else's personality and emotionally annihilated, and they fear being used or humiliated by the person they depend on.

This creates an intimate lifestyle of seeing the loved one as both the "savior" and the "enemy." They pull the loved one in closer and then push him or her away over and over as their needs and fears battle each other. This "dance" is repeated throughout the relationship. People who take on the Caretaker role become the BP/NP's partner in this dance, changing behavioral responses to match what the BP/NP needs at the moment.

THE DANCE OF INTIMATE HOSTILITY

People who are emotionally healthy usually exit a relationship when this push/pull pattern becomes more and more evident. They do not have much need or tolerance for this level of romantic or emotional instability. That is why BP/NPs often have a pattern of many short-term relationships. But when

BP/NPs finds a Caretaker, he or she has found someone to dance to the relationship tune, someone who is adaptable and willing to be intimate and close one minute and who will also feel guilty and responsible enough to hang around when the BP/NP pushes him or her away. Caretakers find that it is extremely difficult to abandon a BP/NP. The Caretaker feels almost a calling to rescue someone who is emotionally hurting. It seems like the right and loving thing to do, but then you can't see any way to leave without devastating the BP/NP.

As a Caretaker for a BP/NP, this dance of "intimate hostility" doesn't seem unfamiliar or bizarre to you. Your need to care for, save, protect, and take responsibility for the BP/NP pulls you deeper into the relationship.

HOW CARETAKERS SEE RELATIONSHIPS

Caretakers have a propensity to be responsible for everything. You may have filled the role of peacemaker, soother, or go-between in your family. Being able to create a calm feeling in an explosive, dysfunctional family; to diffuse intense conflicts; or to have compassion for the BP/NP's pain may be ways that you feel a sense of contribution and value. Like the BP/NP, you may not have received enough attention or validation growing up, or you may have been rewarded for giving up your own wants and needs. You may have pretty low self-esteem, or you may have felt powerful for giving instead of receiving. Maybe your family was highly emotional and you learned how to be a calming influence. Maybe your family never shared or expressed emotions and you are hungry for feelings to be out in the open.

You are highly likely to have come from a dysfunctional family with a parent, sibling, or other relation who is a BP/NP. You may have been trained from early childhood to take care of a dysfunctional adult who was depressed, overly anxious, or self-absorbed in some way. You may be someone with a higher-than-normal sense of empathy or compassion. You may have not felt truly heard or emotionally connected as a child and have a strong need to be intensely enmeshed with someone now. Caretakers come to the job from many different backgrounds.

What is common to all Caretakers, however, is a high level of needing to care for others, a willingness to let go of any and all of your own needs, an amazing adaptability, great skill in soothing and calming other people, a lot of internal guilt, high levels of responsibility, and a great dislike of conflict. And finally, to be a Caretaker you must be willing (for whatever reason) to keep interacting with the BP/NP.

WHY THE BP/NP NEEDS THE CARETAKER

Being a Caretaker to a BP/NP is equivalent to being a full-time, unpaid therapist even though the BP/NP is an adult who should be caring for him- or herself. BP/NPs need you to nurture, need you to listen, be caring and concerned, take responsibility for negative feelings, and create a world that is no longer scary. For the BP/NP, this means that the Caretaker must merge emotionally and psychologically with the BP/NP by thinking, feeling, needing, and wanting exactly the same as the BP/NP. This creates a feeling that the two of you are actually one person, so the BP/NP no longer has to feel afraid of being abandoned. However, the BP/NP absolutely has to be the *one* person that both of you become to avoid his or her fear of annihilation. This can then lead to a dissolving of the personality of the Caretaker over time, resulting in increasing depression, anxiety, frustration, confusion, guilt, lowered self-esteem, and even physical stress symptoms.

The most negative feature of being a Caretaker is that the BP/NP desperately needs *you* to be the repository of the BP/NP's overly intense negative, angry, anxiety-laden feelings. BP/NPs have a unique way of "seeing" the world to make it feel safer and less chaotic. It is called *splitting*. Splitting is a defense mechanism that divides the world—all events, people, and feelings—into either *good* or *bad*. In order to feel okay, BP/NPs work hard to keep hold of all the good feelings. They identify with the good feelings. Whenever they have bad feelings, BP/NPs become intensely frightened and fear being overwhelmed by them. So BP/NPs place all the blame and responsibility for those bad feelings on someone/something outside themselves as a way to get rid of those feelings. The BP/NP needs the Caretaker to carry these bad feelings and be responsible for them.

HOW THE CARETAKER ROLE KEEPS THE FAMILY FUNCTIONING

The BP/NP-dominated family is designed to protect the BP/NP. The needs of other family members are not considered in this design. Family members must learn to give into the BP/NP's wants and needs or else pay the price of a temper tantrum, rejection, or emotional or even physical attack. Family members have to take up the slack because of the BP/NP's lack of follow-through, impulsive behaviors, delusional thinking, and confusing, inconsistent, unpredictable, and demanding behaviors. All the rules and roles in the family are designed to make life and daily interactions comfortable for the BP/NP and to take any anxiety and pressure off of him or her.

That means that someone else must bear the daily duty of dealing with the ordinary responsibilities, such as taking care of the needs of the children;

cooking, cleaning, and fixing things around the house; being at fault when something goes wrong; taking the initiative to plan, organize, and follow through with whatever the BP/NP needs; paying bills on time; and anticipating things that will make the BP/NP anxious and upset and making sure these things are avoided.

Usually when you take on the Caretaker role, you think that it is only temporary until the BP/NP gets less stressed, learns to be more mature, gets over the current problem, understands what you need, gets a new job, realizes how mean they are being, and so on. Keep in mind that being the Caretaker is your responsibility to keep until *you* figure out a way to let it go, as BP/NPs are never likely to do any of these things as long as they have you to take care of them. Why should they? Why would they? If you are willing to keep doing everything that needs to be done, why are they going to make any changes?

THE DRAMA TRIANGLE

Stephen Karpman designed the Drama Triangle to outline the way these dysfunctional relationship patterns fit into actual roles.[3] The roles of persecutor, rescuer, and victim appear consistently in drama-dominated, unequal relationships and keep those relationships from maturing and functioning in a healthy, happy, relaxed way. The borderline, narcissist, and Caretaker typically get locked into these three rigid and self-rewarding/self-punishing roles as their only choices.

The *persecutor* has the attitude of "It's all your fault." This role includes blaming, criticizing, anger, rigid demands, rules, and expectations, all aimed at the victim.

The *victim* carries the stance of "Poor me." The person in this role feels hopeless, powerless, overwhelmed, and helpless. The victim refuses to make decisions, take action, or solve problems and remains clueless to what is happening and how to fix it. Thus, the victim never has to take responsibility for anything.

The *rescuer* has the job to "help," whether he or she actually wants to or not. It is a demand, fueled by external and internal guilt, that almost "forces" you to take care of protecting anyone who acts like a victim. This role works to keep the victim dependent while also giving him or her an excuse to fail. The three roles work together, as seen in Figure 2.1.

DRAMA TRIANGLE

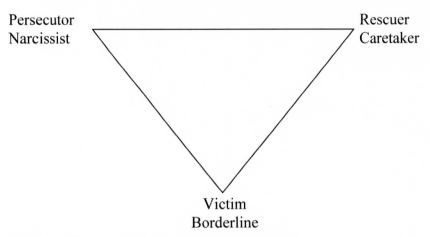

Figure 2.1.   Drama Triangle with Roles Working Together

In a family, there may actually be three people playing the roles, such as father, mother, and child. But often only two people play the roles by switching back and forth. The Caretaker, borderline, and narcissist have their preferred roles as noted above, and they play out implicit, covert agreements to stay in these roles:

> The persecutor and rescuer play out the agreement: "You can't get along without me."
> The victim and rescuer play out the agreement: "We have a special connection."
> The persecutor and victim are playing out the agreement: "If you become what I want, I will love you."

By understanding this triangle of roles and the secret agreements being acted out, it is easier to see why the borderline, narcissist, and Caretaker find one another compatible and how they keep the others in their assigned roles. These roles keep getting played out over and over. However, the problem with this Drama Triangle is that whenever anyone gets uncomfortable in their role, they *only* have either of the other two roles to choose from. The rules in the BP/NP-dominated family are very strict and very rigid, and the Caretaker buys into this dynamic when stepping into being the Caretaker.

A large part of what creates the drama is when the borderline, narcissist, or Caretaker gets fed up with his or her role. Obviously, these roles can become quite tedious and frustrating over time. But with only two other roles to choose from, the results are completely predictable, which is very important to those playing this drama game. Let's look at the possibilities.

When the Caretaker who is in the rescuer role gets fed up with always solving problems and taking care of the borderline or narcissist, you have only two choices, depending on what feelings are dominant. If you are feeling unappreciated and taken advantage of and want to stop being responsible for everything, then you move from being the rescuer and become the victim. Or, if you are frustrated and angry and want someone to blame or someone else to change, then the persecutor role becomes your choice (see Figure 2.2).

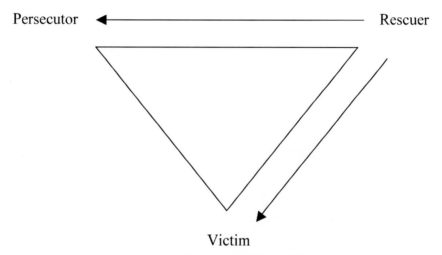

Persecutor ◄─────────────────────────── Rescuer

Victim

Figure 2.2. Drama Triangle with Rescuer as Persecutor or Victim

When the persecutor sees the rescuer threatening to collapse into the victim role, he knows he has pushed and blamed too much and it is upsetting the balance of the triangle. He will feel safest taking on the rescuer role to help the rescuer, who has become a victim, gain enough strength and determination to take back the rescuer role. However, when on the rare occasion the persecutor feels so unappreciated or emotionally or physically drained or when she anticipates being abandoned, the persecutor will very temporarily take on the victim role. Being a victim triggers the partner to go to the rescuer role again. (See Figure 2.3)

Chapter 2

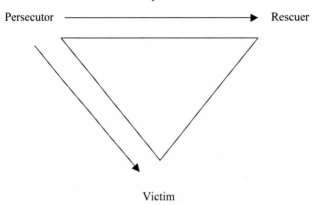

Figure 2.3.   **Drama Trangle with Persecutor as Rescuer or Victim**

Likewise, the victim has only two other choices as well. The person in the victim role can become so angry and frustrated with having no power that he can move into blaming, bullying, demanding, and being a persecutor. However, most people who are used to the victim role don't have enough energy to maintain being a persecutor for very long. They most often revert to a kind of passive-aggressive version of victim/persecutor by being very intractable and stubborn. The other choice the victim has is to act as a rescuer (see Figure 2.4). This will again usually be temporary and most often happens under duress when the rescuer has given up caretaking and the victim is afraid of immanent abandonment.

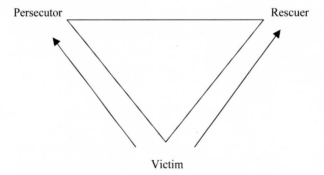

Figure 2.4.   **Drama Triangle with Victim as Persecutor or Rescuer**

The fact that there are only three roles, all dysfunctional, that are allowed in the borderline/narcissist/Caretaker relationship is highly problematic. It becomes clear why having someone be a Caretaker is so necessary to the BP/NP. Two narcissists, both preferring the persecutor role, would constantly be fighting to be in control. Two borderlines in the relationship would each try to outdo the other in being a victim, and no one would be in charge or responsible for anything. The narcissist and borderline can temporarily be a match when the narcissist is willing to be a rescuer while the borderline is being the victim. However, narcissists get exhausted very quickly in the rescuer role and will then revert to being a persecutor, something that the borderline cannot tolerate for very long without emotionally collapsing. A relationship with only a persecutor and a victim degenerates into constant high-level anger, fighting, hysterics, threats of suicide, and often domestic abuse, so this pairing is usually too volatile to be maintained. Someone must always be willing to take on the rescuer role to keep the Drama Triangle in some kind of balance.

This explains more clearly why both the BP and NP need a Caretaker who will fill the rescuer role to keep the relationship functioning. As a Caretaker, you are more adaptable and can move quickly and easily into any of the three roles, whereas the BP and NP work very diligently to stay in their preferred roles. This translates into the unpleasant truth that the Caretaker keeps this Drama Triangle balanced.

As you will see in the next few chapters, the Caretaker is a major dynamic in any relationship with a BP/NP. You are adaptable, competent, and soothing to the BP/NP, and you feel too guilty to leave. Thus, the BP/NP prefers and needs a Caretaker as a partner in order to keep the dance of intimate hostility going and to play the complementing roles in the Drama Triangle.

The following chapters look at the role of Caretaker and how you stay stuck in that role. We will also begin exploring ways to change how you function in relation to the BP/NP so that you can get out of the role.

Chapter Three

What Is a Caretaker?

Every family with a borderline or narcissistic member will have at least one Caretaker, someone who primarily plays the rescuer role. People who are overly empathetic, self-sacrificing, unassuming, deferential, more willing to put other's needs before their own, uncomfortable with conflict, generous, and perfectionistic are more vulnerable to becoming a Caretaker. Someone usually comes to be the Caretaker through volunteering, being tricked or coerced, feeling obligated or guilty, or wanting to fix or "help" the BP/NP. People who get stuck in the Caretaker role for years usually have grown up in a BP/NP-dominated family. If you learned the Caretaker role from childhood because you had a BP/NP parent or sibling, you are more likely to pick a BP/NP spouse because he or she will seem familiar and comfortable.

THE CARETAKER'S JOB

With the borderline person, it is the Caretaker's job to look out for the emotional needs of the BP by doing everything possible to make the BP feel better: Perhaps you help him or her feel safe, you protect him or her from the consequences of his hostile behaviors to others, you make sure nothing upsetting comes into the BP's life, you take over unmet family responsibilities, you make excuses, and you may outright lie to others about the BP so that he or she can appear more socially acceptable.

The Caretaker does much of the same for the narcissist person, but you must also always tell the NP he or she is right; let the NP make all the choices; never upstage or outshine the NP in public; and never do, say, dress, or act in any way that would embarrass or make the NP feel uncomfortable (i.e., never be less than perfect, as this would shed a bad light on the NP). Obviously, this is a huge job for anyone. People who grew up with both borderline and narcissistic parents or siblings suffer double jeopardy and may alternate between relationships with borderline and narcissistic people.

Although Caretakers develop rigid behaviors and ways of thinking to cope with the BP/NP, they seem quite able to function appropriately and adaptably at work, in social situations, and in friendships. You have the ability to interact with others in a variety of ways to meet the expectations of different situations, while BP/NPs do not seem to be able to do so, especially in situations where there is any level of anxiety. It may be that people who become Caretakers do not have the same genetic components as the borderline or narcissist, but at some point you learned to relate to the BP/NP's confused and twisted thoughts, feelings, and behaviors, and this contributes to the dysfunction in the relationship.

As a Caretaker, it is your job to please and take care of the BP/NP first and foremost. To do this, you will have learned to ignore your own needs, become adapted to a highly emotional, tense, and chaotic environment, and become hypervigilant to the BP/NP's emotional reactions. Your job is to do everything that the BP/NP is not willing or able to do, give in to whatever the BP/NP wants, and carefully monitor the family's image in the community.

Although being the Caretaker is a challenging role, you may feel proud of your abilities and skills in keeping the family calm and functioning, and you may have found ways to effectively use these mediating and caretaking skills in the work world. Many Caretakers go into jobs as teachers, nurses, counselors, and managers where these skills are highly valued and in demand.

HOW CARETAKING IS DIFFERENT FROM CODEPENDENCY

Caretaking may sound a lot like codependency. Codependency seems to be a more pervasive set of personality traits that are applied in every aspect of a person's life, including at work, in friendships, at school, in parenting, and in intimate relationships. Codependent behaviors could be described quite similarly to those that Caretakers use. However, most Caretakers take on this role almost exclusively *inside the family* and primarily only with the borderline or narcissist. Often Caretakers are very independent, good decision makers, competent, and capable on their own when not in a relationship with a borderline or narcissist. It is almost as if the Caretaker lives in two different worlds with two different sets of behaviors, rules, and expectations, one set with the BP/NP and another with everyone else. You may even hide your caretaking behaviors from others and try to protect other family members from taking on caretaking behavior, much like child abuse victims try to protect siblings from being abused.

HOW AND WHY YOU LEARNED TO BE A CARETAKER

To become a Caretaker, you need to be highly intuitive of the needs of the BP/NP, intelligent enough to learn the distorted and contradictory rules the BP/NP needs to function, observant enough to keep track of all the nuances of the fast-changing emotional family environment, and creative enough to find ways to calm and appease the BP/NP but also with a low enough self-esteem to not think that you deserve better treatment, more consideration, or equal caring in return. When you become the Caretaker, you take on the role of making the BP/NP feel safe, secure, and loved at all times. In addition, you may also feel it is your job to "teach" the BP/NP to act more appropriately and to help the BP/NP "get better."

The Caretaker role is created by a combination of highly sympathetic and parasympathetic responses, a personality guided primarily by a particular combination of feelings (fear, obligation, and guilt) as well as random and calculated reinforcement by the BP/NP, and a chaotic environment that needs organization to function to meet the basic physical and financial needs of the family.

In addition, Caretakers seem to be more emotionally overresponsive to others than the average person. You have either learned or you just innately respond to the pain of others and see yourself as responsible to take care of that pain. Caretakers are people willing to put their own needs and wants on hold to help and/or please others. They have a tendency to feel hopeless and helpless when overwhelmed and have a great aversion to feeling or expressing anger. They are especially prone to being manipulated by fear, obligation, and guilt, whether coming from others or within yourself.

HOW THE BP/NP MANIPULATES YOU TO STAY IN THE CARETAKER ROLE

Fear, Obligation, and Guilt

Kreger and Shirley, in the *Stop Walking on Eggshells Workbook*, wrote about how the BP/NP uses fear, obligation, and guilt to keep you in a "FOG" of confusion about reality.[1] This FOG tends to pull you into a set of delusional thoughts and behaviors that trap you in the Caretaker role as you try to make life better for the BP/NP.

Fear comes from being unable to predict when the BP/NP will be friendly, loving, demanding, sincere, critical, or furious. Unfortunately, the BP/NP's emotional reactions are random much of the time. You may try very hard to control your own behavior in order to get a predictable reaction from the BP/NP but usually with little success. BP/NPs are emotionally unpredictable to themselves as well as to you. Much of what the BP/NP does is simply due to an emotion that is coursing through him or her at the time and actually has very little to do with you or the situation. But this can be hard to see and very difficult to understand.

For example, BP/NPs often require their loved ones to say and do things in very particular and exact ways. If you don't get the words or actions exactly right or you stray into topics that are off limits, the BP/NP is likely to discount any positive attempts you have made and explode in anger or retreat into deadly silence.

For example, Barbara recounts,

> I remember once we were expecting company, and I asked my mother, "Are we going to clean the house?" It was just a question, but my mother took it to mean something about her. She slapped me, and then didn't speak to me for a week. She ate her meals in the bedroom. My dad said, "You better apologize to your mother." So even though it seemed totally unfair I went to my mother and said, "I'm sorry." I didn't even say what I was sorry for because I actually didn't think I'd done anything wrong, but her face changed instantly into a big smile and I was again in her good graces. None of us ever talked about the incident again.

In some families, the BP/NP erupts into physical violence, but even in families where there are no actual physical attacks, there is still a deep sense of fear that the BP/NP's sudden hatred, anger, or irrational behavior can pop up any time.

Children and spouses of BP/NPs learn not to invite anyone home unexpectedly, never knowing how the BP/NP might be acting or feeling on that day. Even plans made far in advance may not materialize because at the last moment the BP/NP can suddenly go into an uproar.

Irene shares her story.

> On three different occasions my husband invited me to a social or party event for his work. It meant getting a sitter for the kids, getting all dressed up and usually meant driving downtown. I still don't know what would set him off. But every single time, on the way to the party, he would start a fight that would end up with him getting out of the car and walking home. Each time I was stunned and hurt and aghast at his behavior, and I was terribly disappointed. I finally learned it was better to just say that I didn't like going to work functions to avoid the whole insane mess.

Fear is a constant companion in BP/NP families. The sudden outbursts of anger from the BP/NP, the chilling rejection and shunning, the irrational demands, and the inexplicable reasoning from the BP/NP teach family members to be always on guard, to not count on any future plans, and to watch carefully every action, word, gesture, and even facial expression. This creates a "survival" need to please the BP/NP and a sense that you are responsible for the BP/NP's anger, hurt, and hostility.

Obligation sets in when you see the borderline in such pain and anguish from his or her overwhelming fears that it touches your heart or when the narcissist blames you for causing his or her feelings and you feel you must make things right. You take on the obligation to fix the BP/NP's needs. You understand that in this relationship, if anything is going to change, you will have to make it happen. Caretakers frequently keep hoping for things to get better with the BP/NP, and you may keep trying for years to make things better. However, the BP/NP rarely does get any better, so you begin taking up the slack, becoming more and more obligated to keep the family functioning. Although BP/NPs can function pretty well in some situations, they often do especially poorly at home in their personal relationships, and they often have very contradictory behaviors that may not make sense to you.

For example, borderline mothers may be fanatic about nutrition yet never clean the house. Narcissistic fathers may produce spectacularly at work but be unable to have a civil conversation at home. In addition, when you complain about these inconsistencies, the BP/NP reverses the responsibility so that you are at fault. This tends to curtail any direct changes demanded of the BP/NP and increases your feeling of obligation to please.

For example, James describes his experience:

> My dad was so incredibly successful at work, and he felt that since he brought in the money, he shouldn't be called on to do anything else. He never once came to any sports events I was in. He didn't even seem to remember that I had scored the winning basket in the tournament. When I would be disappointed or upset with him not participating more in my life, he would tell me I was just being a selfish kid, that he worked hard all day for me, and the least I could do for him was to not complain and whine about coming to some kid's game.

BP/NPs typically feel that it is just too much to ask of them to be responsible for anything they haven't decided to do. They also will leave tasks unfinished when they no longer feel like doing them. Often they believe they are too busy, too stressed, too upset, too angry, or too depressed to deal with all that sort of thing. Anyone who asks them for more than they feel they can do is likely to get verbally abused or made to feel horrible for even considering burdening them with such a request. Therefore, the Caretaker takes on more and more responsibility and family obligations because the BP/NP just won't do them, and it is way too much work to even ask the BP/NP to do his or her share.

Caretakers learn to not ask for emotional support, take on the extra responsibilities that the BP/NP dropped, and think of the BP/NP's feelings before their own. The punishment for failing to care for the BP/NP's emotional needs before your own is family chaos and sometimes total emotional disintegration of the BP/NP. The greater your need for approval, order, or emotional predictability, the more likely you are to be pulled into overfunctioning as a Caretaker. As obligations pile up, you find yourself feeling resentment, depression, and a sense of helplessness and hopelessness as well as exhaustion.

Guilt is another way BP/NPs keep you caretaking them. BP/NPs cannot stand to accept that they ever make mistakes, make bad judgments, have caused anyone to feel bad, or need to make changes in themselves—except, that is, when they are occasionally overwhelmed by feeling all these things a thousandfold. BP/NPs are *never* responsible, or they are *totally* responsible. These extreme reactions to everyday problems create an ongoing family chaos of blame and denial as well as a sense of confusion and distortion as to what is real. It also makes it difficult to do any sort of effective problem solving.

Amazingly, it is because BP/NPs actually feel so totally anguished about any mistake that they cannot recognize or own their mistakes for fear that all their self-hatred will come to the forefront of their awareness. By blaming others for everything that goes wrong (including the BP/NP's own uncomfortable internal feelings), the BP/NP is able to avoid his or her own hostile, internal self-judgment. This blame causes a feeling in the family that no one is ever good enough and that you, the Caretaker, somehow must fix the BP/NP's pain. You may even feel guilt for feeling happy while the BP is so unhappy. This can pressure you to try even harder to make the BP/NP happy. The BP/NP uses fear, obligation, and guilt to manipulate and pressure you to stay functioning in the Caretaker role.

Delusions

A *delusion* is a strongly and adamantly held belief that has no basis in fact or is even contrary to fact. BP/NPs use a lot of internally created, delusional explanations for how they came to feel so terrible. To them, their feelings are the actual truth of reality despite any facts to the contrary. If they feel a certain way, BP/NPs will assume that someone or something outside of themselves *made* them feel that way. As the closest family member, the Caretaker is usually the one who must take the blame for how the BP/NP is feeling. The BP/NP often uses the phrase, "You made me feel . . ." Since the BP/NP's feelings actually come from his or her own emotional reactions and internal chemistry, this can feel very confusing to you. The more confused you feel, the more vulnerable you are to discounting your own judgment, believing that you really are the cause, and going along with the BP/NP to keep the peace.

If the BP/NP feels better in response to what you do, you can get caught up in thinking that you *do* have the power to make the BP/NP feel worse or better. You buy into his or her delusion. This can reinforce you into continuing in the role of Caretaker. But the more you believe the delusion that you are responsible for how the BP/NP feels, the worse you feel about yourself. This leads to lower and lower self-esteem, more trying on your part to fix what cannot be fixed, and more entrapment in the Caretaker role.

Rigid Family Rules and Roles

BP/NPs often hold an extremely perfectionist standard for the behavior of others while expecting very few or no consequences for their own behaviors. This unfair yet rigid application of rules and roles by the BP/NP is treated as normal by everyone in the family. Healthier members of the family are expected to be totally committed to protecting and caring for the BP/NP's feelings and needs. The BP/NP may be irresponsible, abusive, sarcastic, self-centered, and mean, but you are required to make the BP/NP feel better, never disagree with him or her, and never tell people outside the family anything negative about the BP/NP.

Family members are often cast into specific roles—such as the social one, the responsible one, the funny one, or the Caretaker—and behaviors outside those narrow roles may be denied or even punished. If you take over a certain responsibility for the BP/NP, you may never be allowed to let that chore go, even for important reasons, because no one else can or will be allowed to take it over. Elderly BP/NPs often still expect their adult children to obey them the same way they did when they were 12 years old.

This rigidity of rules and roles makes the BP/NP-dominated family particularly unable to solve problems effectively or to respond to change. It also reinforces the belief that change is bad, dangerous, and frightening. As a Caretaker, you might interpret this to mean that being more assertive, expressing your own wants and needs, or leaving your Caretaking role would be ruinous to the BP/NP and the whole family. It certainly would change the dynamics of the family profoundly.

Blaming the Caretaker

The BP/NP designates the Caretaker to take on the blame for everything that goes wrong and is adept at blaming others for their behaviors, as in the following:

> You made me feel . . .
> If you hadn't said it that way, I wouldn't have . . .
> If you hadn't done. . . , I wouldn't have . . .
> You did it too.

You are so rejecting [in response to any request for kinder behavior].
You know I love you, even when I am cheating on you.
You are always mean and hurtful to me, so I'm doing it right back.

When you are continually blamed for what happens, you can come to feel that you actually are responsible. This responsibility can give you a sense of hopelessness and helplessness. On the other hand, it can also make you think that you have the power to change things. You may feel that it is all in your hands and that everyone is relying on you. This is another delusion. Taking the blame is not a way to gain power in the relationship with the BP/NP. It is only a road to futility. The BP/NP has too much emotional investment in not changing to ever start taking responsibility based on you telling them to.

Mystification

The BP/NP also mystifies (confuses) your picture of reality by inconsistent and crazy-making comments and behaviors such as the following:

The BP says, "I hate you and I can't stand to look at you," but the BP won't leave you alone.
The day after a rage, the BP acts like nothing ever happened.
The BP describes himself as a "positive" person.
The NP screams, "Don't you raise your voice to me."
After the BP tells you how uncaring you've been, she wants to be comforted.
The NP parent sets the behavioral expectations for the child so high that the child inevitably fails and feels devalued.
The BP calls eight times to tell you that she's giving you the silent treatment.

BP/NPs do not see things from an objective or reality perspective. They have a feeling, act on it for their own benefit, and then make up a plausible reason for why they did it. The reason doesn't have to make sense in reality because the BP/NP doesn't operate in reality. The BP/NP's motives and conclusions make sense only to the BP/NP. When you try to make BP/NPs see that their thinking doesn't make sense, they can talk in circles until you are totally confused about what is going on. This can leave you feeling that *you* are crazy. The more you try to make BP/NPs see reality, the more resistant they become.

Giving as a Requirement to Receive

When you are in relationship with a BP/NP, you begin to believe that unless you please and care for him or her, you will not get loved or cared for yourself. Love and affection are intermittent at best, and this can leave you feeling desperately needy for love. Children in BP/NP families learn to care for the parent in an attempt to get cared for themselves. At any rate, your needs will never be appropriately or sufficiently responded to in this relationship. This leaves you feeling always in need of the BP/NP's attention. Keeping your needs unmet is a powerful way to keep you trying to be good enough to get attention and love from the BP/NP. It locks you into trying harder, doing more, and putting up with the demands of the BP/NP in order to, it is hoped, get some of your needs met. But as the Caretaker, you will always be on the short end of the receiving.

Emotional Merging

BP/NP families work on the premise of "all for one." However, that *one* has to be the BP/NP. You are expected to think like the BP/NP, feel like him or her, and share the same opinions and behaviors as he or she has. Differences cannot be tolerated and are attacked by the BP/NP because to disagree means to the BP/NP that he or she is wrong, bad, or shameful. Merging into an amoeba-like oneness is the only tolerable state for the BP/NP, and the *one* must be them. It is very difficult in this situation to know who *you* are, what *you* think, or what *you* actually feel. You start thinking that you and the BP/NP really are the same person. His or her needs are your needs, and his or her feelings should be your feelings.

Lack of Intimacy

Because of the demand for everyone to be the same in the BP/NP family, intimacy is completely absent. Intimacy does not occur when everyone must be alike. Your need for intimacy, however, is a deep human craving and is part of your life purpose. People in BP/NP relationships have both a great longing for intimacy because it is missing and a great fear of it because it would disrupt the pseudointimacy of the "all is one" feeling of *merging* that they believe keeps everyone emotionally safe and accepted. Basically, merging is exchanged for real intimacy. Since you very likely don't have much idea what real intimacy feels like, you are not likely to want to give up merging for the unknown.

Fear of Intimacy

True intimacy is really a mutual sharing of one person's most personal and individual thoughts, feelings, and beliefs with another, the assumption being that the two people are unique and different and that the sharing is a test of love and acceptance of each for the other. Intimacy solidifies your sense of being seen and accepted for who you really are. It is risky because the other person may not agree with you and may not like everything about you. But acceptance based on differences is extremely powerful, bonding, and positive. So why do Caretakers keep falling into relationships with BP/NPs or stay in those relationships with no realistic hope of being more intimate? Do you also fear intimacy? I clearly think so.

Selecting and staying with a BP/NP partner who is not working at getting better or going from one BP/NP relationship to another makes it highly unlikely that you will ever have an intimate relationship. The relationship with a BP/NP is not about being emotionally close, nor is it about having your innermost feelings and needs responded to. Primarily, it is the *hope* or *fantasy* of being seen, heard, and responded to that keeps Caretakers in the relationship. Why would you keep getting involved with BP/NP partners based on hope and fantasy and cutting yourself off from other, more healthy relationships? I think it is a deep fear that you are not good enough to be accepted as you are.

In addition, being in a long-term relationship with a BP/NP results in a lot of anxiety about intimacy. Although you may want more intimacy, your experiences with the BP/NP have also made you fear closeness. Closeness in the BP/NP family is far from fun. In fact, it is subtly or overtly dangerous because the rules about merging and being exactly alike result in the elimination of everyone's identity, except the BP/NP's. The repetitive pattern of many years of being involved with a BP/NP keeps you away from true intimacy and can lead you to feel much too vulnerable in normal relationships.

WHY WOULD ANYONE WANT TO BE A CARETAKER?

Being a Caretaker can lead to a heady feeling of being a strong, wise, and needed person. Playing this role as a child can make you feel equal or even superior to the adults in the family. Unfortunately, being a Caretaker means learning to be overly vigilant of the needs of others and pretty much ignorant of your own feelings, needs, and reactions, but you may not even notice that since you are so focused on the BP/NP.

As a Caretaker, you have developed at least a limited sense of individuality or sense of self. Most often, this self functions pretty well in the outside world. In the world of work, you may be highly conscientious and helpful, do a thorough job, and be seen as a valued employee. However, Caretakers have a tendency to "burn out" because of overdoing, continual worry about being liked, and the constant striving to be perfect. In spite of that, the work world makes sense to you. It is logical and predictable and feels safer than personal relationships, and it rewards you for being functional. Being able to learn functional roles in the world of work and school has had a tremendous impact on your becoming a healthier person.

In personal intimate relationships, however, your sense of self may be much more vulnerable, fragile, and unclear than you realize. This makes you more easily victimized and manipulated by a BP/NP. You forgive the BP/NP over and over, take on more and more responsibility for the relationship, and, when nothing gets any better, end up feeling used, exhausted, angry, and confused. You believe that somehow if you just did the "right thing," you would be able to help the BP/NP become happier and more satisfied, and then the BP/NP would show you the love that you want. Whenever the borderline acts normally, you become immensely elated, believing time and time again that now "everything will be better," only to be let down when he or she returns to dysfunctional thinking and behaving again. This makes you vulnerable to overfunctioning in relationships and putting up with a partner who is severely underfunctioning. When the narcissist does something especially thoughtful, you think that he or she has "turned a corner" and matured and will now be the loving partner you want. It seems so logical. But none of these changes lasts longer than a few days or hours.

The BP/NP has had many rejections in love before you came along. Others have experienced the BP/NP's controlling and even selfish behaviors in relationships and have left. You, however, see the clues but don't leave. Instead, you feel drawn in, you may feel the BP/NP *needs* you, and you may feel rewarded for your rescuer responsibilities. You feel a level of excitement and hope. You see a match. At first, this seems like a comfortable relationship. To you, nothing seems particularly amiss. Somehow you know all the corresponding moves in this relationship dance, and you feel like you have a wonderful chance to make life better for the BP/NP. However, this is not intimacy; rather, it is the familiar Drama Triangle of victim/persecutor/rescuer.

WHY DIDN'T YOU BECOME A BP/NP?

Why did you end up being a Caretaker instead of a BP/NP yourself? It appears that certain people are more emotionally in jeopardy of becoming BP/NPs than others.[2] People who are emotionally intense, more sensitive to stress, more easily confused by double messages, and overwhelmed by illogical interactions or passive-aggressive behaviors have greater tendencies to develop borderline personality disorder or narcissistic personality disorder. There also appears to be a biological factor in borderline personality disorder—perhaps genetic damage or infection in utero or in early childhood and/or some form of high sensitivity to stress that predisposes a person to develop borderline personality disorder. They may also have a greater propensity to dissociate, that is, leave their bodies and let their minds wander in a fantasy world to avoid dealing with the intolerable stress of the present situation.

Physical or sexual abuse can push a vulnerable child over the edge to posttraumatic stress disorder and/or personality disorders. The double messages, reversal of parent and child roles, and extreme emotionality of BP/NP families have a hugely damaging effect on children already prone to being overwhelmed by stress. If you grew up in such a family, you would have learned the dysfunctional relationship patterns and been affected, but not in the same way as the BP/NP.

You developed in the opposite direction of the BP/NP. You became overly responsible and caring of others. You also became vulnerable to overdoing, overworrying, and being overwhelmed in intimate relationships. Unlike the BP/NP, you find it hard to identify your anger and often act passively in situations where you need to stand up for yourself. People who become Caretakers also seem to have greater-than-normal levels of anxiety and depression that result from the bizarre and distorted interactions with the BP/NP. In the next chapter, we look at some of the common distortions about life and relationships that keep you locked into this rigid role as a Caretaker.

Chapter Four

Caretaker Involvement Levels

Not all people who become Caretakers take on the role at the same level of involvement. Some get immersed and totally focused on the BP/NP, giving up nearly all sense of their own individuality. Others move their attention to the BP/NP during times of emotional uproar and then can move back to their own wants, needs, and feelings much of the rest of the time. Some Caretakers may cut off connection entirely. The more intensely involved in being a Caretaker that you are with the BP/NP, the more work it is going to be to move out of that role and into a healthy life where you are no longer focused on taking care of the BP/NP. Check your score on the Caretaker Test in the appendix to get an idea of which category most fits for you. The following five categories in Figure 4.1 represent caretaking from most to least involved.

Caretaker Levels of Involvement

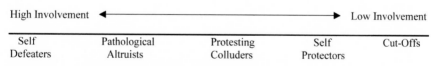

High Involvement				Low Involvement
Self Defeaters	Pathological Altruists	Protesting Colluders	Self Protectors	Cut-Offs

Figure 4.1.   Caretaking from Most to Least Involved

SELF-DEFEATERS

Self-defeating Caretakers consistently select relationships that are rejecting and humiliating. They have an intense desire to please others—even to the level of needing desperately to please people they don't even like. Many times, the self-defeating Caretaker was raised by a borderline or narcissist.

Maybe even both parents were BP/NPs. Self-defeating Caretakers have learned to ignore their own needs entirely and may be angry and embarrassed if a need becomes apparent, such as becoming ill, being too tired to function, being emotional in front of others, or disagreeing.

If you are a self-defeating Caretaker, you may find yourself drawn over and over to situations and relationships where you find yourself disappointed, mistreated, unappreciated, or humiliated. Perhaps you consistently get into relationships where you are made fun of, your partner cheats on you, or your partner is already married, keeps breaking up with you, or tells you that he or she doesn't love you or doesn't find you attractive. Yet you continue to pursue the relationship.

You may find that success and the experiences of happiness and hope feel foreign, uncomfortable, and maybe even frightening because for you such positive feelings always end in disaster, disappointment, and failure. You may find yourself rejecting relationships with people who are sweet, gentle, kind, and considerate as being uninteresting, too boring, or not sexually attractive.

Self-defeating Caretakers seem magnetized to taking care of others, whether the other person has asked for help or not. They get emotionally involved in other people's problems, may spend money outrageously on others, and help others to the point of exhaustion. At the same time, they reject any and all offers of help for themselves even when they are deeply in need.

> Melanie had been sexually abused by her father since the age of 6 until she finally ran away at 16. She was hospitalized three times for suicide attempts before she was age 24. She had numerous sexual relationships with men who got her hooked on drugs and who were physically abusive. Eventually, she quit drugs, got a job, and attended community college. There she met and married a kind, understanding man. With the help of therapy, she started feeling better about herself. However, she would often complain about how boring and stupid her husband was for being married to her. She would have a day or two of feeling good and then go into a prolonged depression, saying that she knew she would never be happy. She would buy expensive gifts for people she barely knew, write papers for other students, but not leave enough time to finish her own assignments. She quit therapy after only a few months, saying that she could no longer afford even the reduced fee. When asked what the problem was, she said that she and her husband were having to file bankruptcy because of the cost of the anniversary party she was giving her father and his third wife.

Melanie kept struggling to pull herself out of the pain and hurt from her childhood, but for every step she took forward, she would take two or three back. Melanie found it hard to take care of herself because she was always trying to please and take care of others, even people who abused, belittled, and rejected her. She wouldn't even allow herself any enjoyment of her relationship with her husband because he was "too nice."

Do you find yourself always wishing for things to be better, for people to be nicer, wishing to be appreciated, but always picking friends and ending up in situations where you are treated badly? Do you find it hard to get up energy to do nice things for yourself, but you will work tirelessly to take care of others? Does it make you feel guilty to buy something for yourself, but you easily spend money you don't have on special treats for others? Do you get depressed when you finally achieve a goal you have wanted to reach? Have you ever had an "accident" or gotten sick just after feeling really good or getting a new job or starting a new relationship? Do you feel consistently unappreciated, rejected, or overwhelmed? Do you find you actually feel more comfortable and safe when you are depressed?

These are the signs of the self-defeating Caretaker. This is the most intense level of caretaking. You may find it hard to imagine success and happiness for yourself, yet you feel intense pain for others when they are not happy. This level of Caretaking can create depression, a sense of being overwhelmed, and sometimes emotional exhaustion, financial ruin, and a complete loss of your self-esteem. It will take work and a lot of help and support from others to move yourself out of this self-defeating mode of living, but don't you really, in your heart, want to give up your life of being a doormat, a personal slave, or a drudge for the benefit of others who don't really care about you?

PATHOLOGICAL ALTRUISM

The next level down from Caretaker involvement is pathological altruism.[1] At this level, you find joy in giving to others. You like making others feel happy. You often surprise others with thoughtful gifts and doing favors. However, you may find it uncomfortable and a little embarrassing when others do the same for you. You don't know how to accept thanks, or you may brush off gratitude or blush when others are appreciative. It may take you quite awhile before you notice that your needs, wants, and feelings are not paid much attention by the BP/NP. He or she doesn't seem to notice when you are tired or need a kind word or a neck rub like you would do for him or her. You may begin to feel that you are being taken for granted and unappreciated. Although you may notice some internal anger about this unfairness, it is probably very hard for you to share this feeling with anyone. You might tell a friend that you are upset about the BP/NP but never tell the BP/NP that you are angry or that anything is wrong.

You may notice the following pattern in many of your relationships. When you first like someone, you are very enthusiastic, excited, and delighted. You go out of your way to do nice things for the person, to please him or her, and to be extra kind. Your expectation is that he or she will do the same for you. However, you probably don't notice the subtle ways that you actually discourage others from giving you the same loving treatment. As the relationship progresses, you find yourself giving more and more and the other person giving less and less. You start feeling used and unappreciated, and you begin seeing the other person as a "taker." You become disillusioned with the relationship and start pulling away and may quit talking to or liking the other person altogether. If you feel compelled to stay in the relationship, you may start feeling hurt, disappointed, and frustrated with the other person. Occasionally, when you feel especially upset, you may lash out and say what you are feeling, but immediately you find yourself feeling profoundly ashamed and guilty for "being so mean." You then apologize and begin trying to be even nicer, more thoughtful, and more giving but still without regard to what you are getting out of the relationship.

The results of persistent pathological altruism are depression and feeling inadequate and disappointed in others and in life. You may develop a significant number of physical aches and pains because holding in what you really think and feel causes a lot of tension to build up in your body. You may especially feel pain in your head, neck, shoulders, and back. Chronic low-level depression is common when you ignore your own needs and feelings for long periods of time.

Using the ideas in this book will be extremely helpful to you in dealing with these symptoms. Following the suggestions can help you move from being a sacrificing server to a whole, healthy person who can be caring of yourself as well as others.

PROTESTING COLLUDERS

In the middle of the continuum are the Caretakers who may never have been a Caretaker in other relationships. You may find yourself stuck in the relationship with the BP/NP because you are a good-hearted person, caring, understanding, and rather confused by the strange behavior of the BP/NP. You have a strong tendency to feel sorry for the borderline's pain or lured into the excitement and fun that the narcissist offers early in the relationship.

Protesting colluders tend to be extremely loyal and expect high levels of commitment from themselves. However, you are surprisingly willing to be forgiving and overly tolerant of the lack of commitment and participation by the BP/NP. You may have had one BP/NP in your family growing up, and you probably have had a friend or two who would fit the BP/NP description.

The main element that protesting colluders share is low self-esteem in the relationship. This may be hard to recognize because you probably have a moderate to high self-esteem at work and in friendships. You may feel strongly that you deserve better treatment and consideration from the BP/NP, but you don't actually do much to make that happen. You collude with the BP/NP to protect the relationship from dissolving, usually by your own perfectionistic demands that you be loyal to the BP/NP no matter how he or she treats you.

Protesting colluders are the most vulnerable to being tricked by the BP/NP's promise to change. You think that if the BP/NP acts nicer one time, the relationship will start moving in a more positive direction and that everything will improve. Surprisingly, you can be tricked over and over without any substantive changes by the BP/NP. Your sense of loyalty demands that you be continually forgiving and hopeful even without any real evidence.

Your participation in the relationship is not without protest, however. Protesting colluders are the most likely Caretakers to complain about the behaviors of the BP/NP. You try to make demands that the BP/NP treat you better, and you may spend a huge amount of time and energy trying to prove to the BP/NP that you deserve better treatment. You especially try to use logic with the BP/NP to convince him or her that you are right and the BP/NP should just "do it your way." However, nothing in the relationship ever does change because you are not willing to take the difficult step of enforcing consequences on the BP/NP for his or her neglectful, selfish, and uncaring behavior toward you.

You collude with the BP/NP to maintain the status quo, and, at the same time you are angry, protesting, and demanding that the relationship change. You have the ability to apply all of the skills outlined in the following chapters. Your main struggle will be in setting limits and boundaries with the BP/NP and convincing *yourself* that you deserve to be treated lovingly and caringly.

SELF-PROTECTORS

Self-protecting Caretakers have learned to step away from the drama with the BP/NP. You set limits and refuse to interact with the BP/NP when he or she is being manipulative and demanding. By thinking ahead, you plan your interactions with the BP/NP to avoid falling into the persecutor/victim/rescuer game. You work consistently to be aware of your own thoughts, needs, and beliefs in order to maintain a separate sense of yourself. However, all of this awareness takes a lot of planning and energy.

You may feel like you are being mean, uncaring, and manipulative toward the BP/NP. Every decision and behavior on your part has to be well chosen to keep yourself out of the emotional drama that surrounds the BP/NP. You find that it takes a lot of attention and work to avoid being angry at yourself or the BP/NP. You see that the relationship with the BP/NP can rarely be relaxed and easy because you are is always being pushed by the BP/NP to conform to his or her needs, wants or demands, and you must always be on the lookout to keep your sense of self intact.

Self-protecting Caretakers work on changing the distortions in their own thinking, feelings, and behavior rather than the distortions in the BP/NP. You have come to understand that expecting the BP/NP to change is futile. Being kind and considerate and at the same time setting boundaries and limits on the BP/NP is a constant challenge, but this is the primary goal of the self-protecting Caretaker. Every skill and technique described in the following chapters will be helpful in reaching your goals. As these new skills become second nature, you will find that you spend less energy on avoiding caretaking because it is much more enjoyable and rewarding to not be in that role.

CUTOFFS

People who fall into this category may still be afraid of falling into the Caretaker role and adamantly refuse to give into that behavior. You may have been stuck in the Drama Triangle with a BP/NP in the past, been forced into a Caretaker role as a child, or gotten out of a disastrous relationship with a BP/NP and have some fear of being pulled back into the role of Caretaker. Cutoff behavior does not denote noncaretaking. This is still a reaction to being vulnerable and fearful of being pulled back into the Caretaker role. You may find that you know you don't want to be a Caretaker but also be anxious that the BP/NP or others could use guilt, pity, or manipulation to force you back into that role.

The result is that you fight your Caretaker tendencies by doing everything possible to avoid any interaction with the BP/NP who was or still is in your family. You may have decided to have no contact even for holidays or visits. You may be making sure that the BP/NP doesn't know how to contact you. You may even pretend that the BP/NP doesn't even exist by pretending that you were never married, that you don't have an NP brother, or that your BP parent has died.

The difficulty of being cutoff rather than being healed from caretaking is that you still feel that vulnerability to being hooked or forced back into the Caretaker role again. This could easily happen if the BP/NP surfaces back into your life because of children you share or if the BP/NP is a dying parent or a sibling in trouble. You may also find that even if you choose to cutoff, that deep-seated fear of getting hooked into the role again has a tendency to make you avoid other intimate relationships, even positive ones. Facing your fears about being caught up in caretaking again can be greatly helped by the suggestions and skills in the following chapters.

NONCARETAKERS

A true noncaretaker very rarely gets caught into the drama games of the BP/NP. Noncaretakers do not feel a need to protect, save, feel sorry for, or understand the borderline. They do not feel extra special, dazzled, or even interested in the over-the-top attention and self-importance that the narcissist displays. Instead, noncaretakers see the BP/NP as strange, odd, and annoying. The noncaretaker's typical reaction is to move away from interacting with the BP/NP because the usual give-and-take and the normal boundaries of a healthy relationship are constantly being breached. This is uncomfortable and irritating for a noncaretaker who picks up very quickly that the interaction is not relaxed, comfortable, or rewarding.

When noncaretakers find themselves in frequent contact with a BP/NP, they will usually try to ignore the BP/NP and limit their contact as much as possible. When one client of mine found herself sharing an office with a BP/NP, she started working in the library, documented the offending behavior with human resources, and requested a move. Many of the skills suggested in later chapters give ideas of how to avoid getting caught up in interactions with a BP/NP.

If you are now a Caretaker at some level, you may never entirely become a noncaretaker. But this description should give you some ideas about what noncaretaking looks like. This book will also help you learn that being a Caretaker is not the same as being a nice person. Caretaking doesn't mean that you are more caring or more understanding or especially kind. Caretaking a BP/NP comes from a mix of dysfunctional and distorted emotions, thoughts, and behaviors that lead to self-destruction and eventual disability, as outlined in the next several chapters.

Chapter Five

Emotional Distortions of Caretakers

The BP/NP functions on a whole set of distortions in his or her emotions, thoughts, behaviors, sense of self, and relationships, as discussed in chapter 1. As a Caretaker, you, too, get drawn into patterns of distortions along with the BP/NP. You may use healthy and realistic guidelines at work and in most friendships but find that with the BP/NP, your emotions, ideas, beliefs, actions, sense of who you are, and how you function in that relationship are very confused and contradictory. Because the BP/NP usually controls the roles, rules, emotional tone, and acceptable behaviors in your relationship, you can find yourself having all kinds of reactions that you would not necessarily have with others. Let's look at the common emotional distortions in which many Caretakers find themselves stuck.

EMOTIONAL UNDERREACTIVITY

Although you may be used to a lot of emotionality from the BP/NP, your role as Caretaker is to remain calm, organized, rational, and unemotional. However, inside, you may have high anxiety, sadness, self-critical shame, and even hidden rage and inner guilt, but it is unlikely that you will show that to the BP/NP or anyone else. The BP/NP is often very intolerant of anyone else expressing emotion. So you have learned to ignore or repress your own feelings. You may not even know what your feelings are when you are in the presence of the BP/NP because you are so focused on him or her. You may also have come to despise being outwardly emotional because it is too much like the BP/NP. Even shedding tears in public may feel humiliating to you.

However, not showing emotion does not mean that you have no strong feelings. It simply means that you have trained yourself to deny your own responses in favor of paying attention to the BP/NP.

EMOTIONAL MINIMIZATION

In general, Caretakers tend to be overly tolerant of the emotionally charged behavior of the BP/NP—sometimes acting as if the BP/NP's outburst, anger, or emotional attack isn't even happening. The ultimate effect of minimizing the BP/NP's inappropriate, out-of-line, and bizarre behavior is to deny that it has any effect on you. But it is important for you to see that these behaviors do, in fact, affect you.

You tend to inwardly criticize the awfulness of your own emotional reactions, yet you significantly downplay the emotionality of the BP/NP. This results in *your* colluding with the BP/NP to maintain the relationship just as it is. However, this leaves you stuck at the mercy of being emotionally manipulated and abused by the BP/NP. You can't get out of the Caretaker experience of being a doormat until you can acknowledge the real level of emotional reaction going on in the borderline, in the narcissist, and in yourself.

EMOTIONAL OVERREACTIVITY

When you deny your wants and feelings over and over, try to smooth things over for the BP/NP too long, and force yourself to stay calm even when you feel furious, it is not surprising that *you* eventually blow up, start an argument, or feel like you just can't stand a certain irritating situation one moment longer. Then, seemingly out of the blue, you explode. This can be startling and surprising to you and to others. The experience that triggers your overreaction may actually be fairly small compared to many other things that have recently happened, but you can end up thinking you are as crazy as the BP/NP seems. This sudden strong reaction may leave you feeling intensely embarrassed or shameful. Suddenly, you see yourself behaving like the BP/NP, and this can feel horrifying. These explosions in Caretakers may happen only once or twice a year, but they are very memorable and embarrassing to you.

Feelings can't go forever being shut down. Feelings that are invalidated, denied, and ignored can cause a physical tension that can explode with little or no warning. For you to be out of control can be very disconcerting and embarrassing. Since it is so rare, it can trigger an onslaught of self-criticism, self-loathing, and self-attack.

Both you and the BP/NP feel the huge unbalance when you have had a sudden emotional overreaction. Having emotionally unresolved needs of your own is breaking the rules. Typically, you will feel guilt (perhaps along with some relief) at your "inappropriate" display of your emotional needs. And frequently, BP/NPs latch on to this display of emotion in Caretakers to "prove" that you are just like them.

Caretakers get their emotions back in line very quickly through self-criticism, self-punishment, self-put-downs, and other forms of self-attack. This does work to shut your emotions down again. However, this self-attack simply continues the pattern of emotional over- and underreaction that keeps you locked into a relationship with the BP/NP.

FEAR OF ANGER

You might notice that you have a great fear of dealing with anger in yourself or others. Your own anger might make you feel like a bad person. Other people's anger can be very frightening and even trigger an internal surge of self-hatred, depression, and guilt at feeling that you caused their upset.

Fear of anger puts you at the mercy of the BP/NP who has no fear of expressing his or her feelings and even blaming them on you. As long as you are afraid of anger, you will find yourself stuck in the Caretaker role.

I DON'T NEED ANYTHING

Caretakers consistently say they are not needy. After all, you can't be the rescuer if you have needs, too. You see the BP/NP as the needy person, and certainly he or she demonstrates neediness in a continuous fashion. However, Caretakers also have very deep and unfilled needs. You, however, deal with this deficit by turning your attention toward taking care of the BP/NP's needs. This distracts your attention from yourself, but it actually ends up increasing your level of unmet needs.

When you look inside, you will see that you have a secret and intense desire to be seen, heard, cherished, and nurtured just like everyone else. However, you may not become aware of these needs until you are exhausted, ill, overwhelmed, or completely beyond your ability to cope. It may be only at this desperate point that you acknowledge your needs, and then they come thundering down on you. Everyone has these needs, and you have a right to ask for these needs to be met by your partner.

Unacknowledged feelings and needs can overwhelm you with a tidal wave of intensity if they are ignored for too long. When this happens, you are very likely to lash out with anger at the BP/NP for taking you for granted, for being selfish, and for lacking in human compassion for your needs. This lashing out and anger are really ways to cover up your feelings of shame for having these emotions at all. Typically, within a few minutes or hours, you bring yourself "back to normal" and again forget or ignore that this vulnerability ever surfaced.

This explosion of neediness and vulnerability is often interpreted by you and the BP/NP as evidence that both of you are alike. Keep in mind that your show of neediness happens once or twice a year and that the BP/NP's neediness happens dozens of times a day. This pattern of denying your needs and then being overwhelmed by neediness keeps you in the Caretaker role and always on the verge of desperation.

EMOTIONAL RESPONSE VERSUS THOUGHT RESPONSE

Caretakers are especially vulnerable to an emotional response rather than a thinking response in situations where they feel *guilt*. Since the BP/NP's most common response to the world is to blame others for his or her feelings, you are in for a lot of guilt feelings in these relationships.

You may be very confused about how you got to feeling so guilty, but you also find it enormously difficult to let go of guilt. However, as long as you feel guilty, you will feel responsible to try to fix or save the relationship with the BP/NP. Again, this keeps you being a Caretaker and a rescuer.

Caretakers do not let go of any relationships easily; you will try everything possible, including giving up your own feelings and needs, to save the relationship with the BP/NP. You may feel that letting go of this relationship is a personal failure. You may have a mystical feeling that if you had been good enough, you could have made it work by your sheer determination. This is emotional reasoning rather than reality thinking.

FEAR OF FAILURE

Why does any possibility of your relationship with the BP/NP ending make you feel so anxious? Could it be that being in a relationship (even a dysfunctional one) gives you hope that someone else will meet your needs, that is, the needs that you don't acknowledge but have anyway? Could it be your fear of feeling like a failure? Could it be that it would prove you're not lovable? Does it feel like being abandoned?

In fact, most Caretakers who are not in a relationship function extremely well. You are emotionally healthier, take better care of your own needs, and enjoy friendships and social activities that you don't have time for when with the BP/NP. The belief that you have to have the BP/NP in your life to function and be happy is an emotional distortion. Believing that you absolutely must be successful in this relationship or else you are a failure is another.

FEELING UNLOVABLE

There is a deep fear of being unlovable that resides in most Caretakers. You are often more emotionally dependent on your relationships than you realize.

Feeling deeply unlovable keeps you believing that you are "lucky" that any-one would want you. As long as you dislike and disapprove of yourself, you will need someone else to prove to you that you are lovable by his or her attention and need. When the person from whom you are seeking that ap-proval is as mentally and emotionally dysfunctional as the BP/NP is, you can never fully get that validation. It can leave you always being hopeful of convincing the BP/NP by your good deeds, your kindness, your tolerance of his or her problems, and your willingness to give up reciprocity. This keeps you stuck caretaking the BP/NP yet never succeeding.

These emotional distortions are trapping you into staying a Caretaker. You are being trapped by your own misreading of emotions in the BP/NP and yourself, your unmet emotional needs, and your fears of anger, failure, and being unlovable. These emotional distortions and the distortions in the following chapters are at the true core of what keeps you stuck as a Caretak-er, always trying to rescue the BP/NP instead of yourself.

Chapter Six

Thought Distortions of Caretakers

The most common thought distortions that Caretakers use include all-or-nothing thinking, perfectionism, the beliefs that logic will convince and that love heals all problems, overresponsibility, too little awareness of your own wants and preferences, a belief that being nice means giving in to whatever your loved one wants, and a lack of ability to see the differences between yourself and the BP/NP.

ALL-OR-NOTHING THINKING

Either I'm completely responsible, or it's all your fault. There are no areas of gray in a BP/NP relationship. The BP/NP constantly uses all-inclusive language, and you probably find yourself doing the same thing with him or her. "Always," "never," and "forever" are words tossed around like they really make sense, which they don't in relationships. Will you always love me? Will you never leave me? These are questions that BP/NPs may ask daily. And you may actually try to respond as if you could actually answer such questions. You buy into this all-or-nothing thinking.

You can't consider options when things have to be all one way forever. With this thinking, any decision can be made only once and must last forever, which is what the BP/NP actually believes and wants. You have the right to have a variety of feelings about things, and you have the right to change your mind. Thinking becomes limited with this all-or-nothing approach, and options become nonexistent. Keeping yourself loyal to this no-win, all-or-nothing thinking simply keeps you trapped in the Caretaker role because you have no options.

PERFECTIONISM

Perfectionism is also a hallmark of BP/NP relationships. Whenever you make a mistake or you are less than perfect, you are blamed, criticized, put down, or made fun of by the BP/NP. Although BP/NPs respond with rage to any expectation of perfectionism from you, Caretakers respond by making greater attempts to do a better job. This demand to be perfect leads to anxiety, a sense of failure, and negative self-attack. "Oh, I am so stupid. Why did I do that? What is the matter with me?" are common Caretaker thoughts.

Do you think that if you put yourself down first, the BP/NP will take compassion on you and not attack or criticize? Expecting perfection in yourself leads you to be too responsive to criticism from the BP/NP. You take his or her criticisms to be facts rather than merely opinions. This gives the BP/NP lots of ammunition to manipulate you. All the BP/NP has to do is criticize you to get what he or she wants.

After Steven's mother had harangued him for 45 minutes about how stupid he was for forgetting his homework the day before, Steven spent the next several days doing everything his mother wanted. He did the dishes and the laundry and was polite and solicitous of her. He expected to get some positive reaction from her, but she ignored him. He felt really used and manipulated when he showed her his new homework assignment with an "A." She just said, "Of course you did fine; you always do." He had thought she actually cared about his success.

Interestingly, Caretakers almost never see themselves as perfectionists because they cannot see themselves as ever being perfect—quite a twist of thinking in itself.

SUPERIOR/INFERIOR: HOW CAN I BE BOTH?

This focus on perfection, combined with accepting the blame for anything that goes wrong, seals the idea that you are totally responsible for making everything right and that you are always a failure. On the one hand, you may feel you are the superior person because you act better and are often more competent than the BP/NP. But you still get the message that you are the inferior or "wrong" person who is to blame. This double message can create long-term confusion, resentment, stress, and hostility, even though you may not be aware of it. In order to follow your assigned role in the family as the Caretaker, you must always be "good" or "nice." You may even be proud of being in the "good person" role. It can give you some sense of superiority, but internally you are likely to still see yourself as damaged and inferior, a failure because things never get better. In addition, you will still be blamed by the BP/NP for anything that makes him or her unhappy no matter what you do.

I'M RESPONSIBLE FOR EVERYTHING

Constantly being blamed leads you to believe that you really are responsible for the feelings and reactions of the BP/NP. Feeling responsible can even seem appealing to some Caretakers because you start thinking that you have control over making things better. Keep in mind that the BP/NP is always the one in control of what goes on in the relationship as long as you remain the Caretaker. You may feel sorry for the borderline or feel needy of the narcissist's attention, so you become more willing to be the responsible one. Unfortunately, being overly responsible does nothing to make your relationship with the BP/NP work better or to create a better life for you; it simply prolongs the way things already are.

SAYING "NO" MEANS NOT BEING NICE

Saying "no" in any form to a BP/NP is rarely received well. The BP/NP's response to being told "no" is most often anger, rage, resentment, criticism, and attack or withdrawal. Before long, you learn to avoid the word "no" in every way possible. Caretakers try hard to be compliant, nice, and agreeable. You learn to bury your own needs, feelings, and opinions, sometimes even from your own awareness. You try to be "nice" to show the BP/NP how you would like to be treated, or you try to prove that you are a good person and not to blame for how awful the BP/NP feels. Again, your self-esteem takes a hit because inside you know that you do not always feel nice. You know that you do not always agree with the BP/NP. You know that you have your own opinions, thoughts, and ideas that are different from the BP/NP's, but you quit expressing them so that you won't "rock the boat." You deny who you are to maintain your Caretaker role.

I DON'T KNOW WHAT I WANT

When you bury your thoughts, ideas, wants, and needs too long, you no longer know what you like, want, or feel. The less you think of your own feelings and opinions, the less discordance you think there will be in the relationship with the BP/NP. you think that if you don't have thoughts or wants, then you will never be in disagreement with the BP/NP. This results in one of the worst distortions in your life. When you do not know what you want, what you feel, or what you really love, you do not have much of a life to call your own. You, as a unique individual, begin to disappear.

Having no strong sense of preferences makes you hard to get to know. When you meet a new person, you may find yourself being quiet, no longer contributing to the conversation or giving opinions. When asked, you may no longer know even what food, movies, or activities you like. You are ceasing to exist.

LOVE HEALS ALL PROBLEMS

Caretakers can be very loving people; that is, you do a lot of loving things for others, you feel strong empathy for the needs of others, you look at nearly everything from the other person's point of view, and you put the other person's wants and opinions ahead of your own. You strongly believe that you must give love in order to get love. You are especially good at the giving. You are not especially good at identifying others who have the ability to give to you.

In healthy relationships, a person will give his or her attention, caring, or thoughts to someone else and then will wait for it to be reciprocated. You tend to give and then become anxious waiting for the other to return the favor, so you give some more and then some more. It becomes especially difficult for you to wait because you can't really ever count on receiving from the BP/NP. So you learn to jump in and give some more rather than waiting. So if the BP/NP can't love, you can do twice the loving. Giving up more and more of yourself to appease and try to heal the BP/NP is self-defeating and doesn't work. It has never worked, and it never will.

When your relationship with the BP/NP becomes painful or unrewarding, your response is to give more, care more, offer more, and love more. You think and hope that by your example the BP/NP will somehow learn to give back to you. It can be quite awhile later before you become aware of being hurt and angry at not getting anything in return. The BP/NP doesn't change by the example of others. He or she is too self-absorbed to notice. Rather than change your thinking based on the lack of results, you make excuses for why the BP/NP isn't responding, and you just keep on giving

Too often, at this point, you start cajoling, begging, and eventually demanding that the BP/NP take on his or her responsibility for loving you back:

"I wouldn't do that to you."
"Look at all I've done for you."
"But you said you would do it."
"Why can't you ever make dinner?"
"I'm always the one who asks you."
"Why don't you ever want to do what I want?"

The BP/NP doesn't understand the concept of reciprocity, that is, the equal back-and-forth, give-and-take of relationships. As a Caretaker, you just keep banging your head against the brick wall of the BP/NP's resistance rather than change your understanding of the BP/NP. You may even find that you can't let go of the relationship with the BP/NP until he or she gives in and starts giving you back the love you have been giving for so long. You are stuck.

NEVER GIVE UP

"Never give up" could be the Caretaker's motto. To you it seems disloyal, selfish, and unloving for you to even consider giving up on any relationship. This belief keeps you being a slave in the relationship to the BP/NP. You see the smallest positive response from the BP/NP as wonderfully giving, which keeps you from exiting. Time after time, this random reinforcement gives you hope. Some Caretakers can't give up even when they see no reciprocal response in the BP/NP for months or years. This insane internal rule that you can never give up also means that you can never quit being a Caretaker as long as you obey it.

THE BP/NP SHOULD BE LOGICAL

It should be clear to you by now that much of the thinking and behavior of the BP/NP is illogical and self-serving and doesn't make sense to anyone else. Healthy people who occasionally interact with the BP/NP just shake their heads, make an angry comment, and move away. You, however, take on the Caretaker task of trying to "teach" the BP/NP to think logically. Caretakers spend enormous amounts of time and energy trying to come up with ways of saying and explaining things to the BP/NP that are more clear, that are more understandable, or that make more sense.

You hang onto the delusional belief that if you could just find the "right way" to explain things, then the BP/NP would see things clearly and the relationship could be healed. Actually, BP/NPs seem to have a random mix of logical and illogical thoughts, which can lead you to think that you have reason for hope. The truth is that the BP/NP is *unable* to consistently respond logically. You may find it hard to believe that this ability just comes and goes in a random manner. However, that is exactly the reality of dealing with a BP/NP. So when you get so caught up trying to be logical, you are trapping yourself in the Caretaker role.

THE BP/NP AND I ARE THE SAME

Another thought distortion that most Caretakers seem stuck on is the belief that you and the BP/NP are alike in how you think, feel, and act. Sometimes you may feel good about this idea (that feeling of oneness), but other times it may scare you, while at other times the BP/NP may threaten you with this idea that you are "just as bad as he or she is."

Kaylee and her NP husband were separated. On a recent visit, they got into an argument. He told her that she never made a contribution to the finances of the family, and she demanded that he look at her W-2. She pushed it in his face and said, "See here." He grabbed her and threw her across the room, breaking her thumb. Kaylee's friend Sandy asked her if she had told the doctor what had happened. "I just told him that I fell," said Kaylee. "It was really my fault that it happened. If I hadn't been so mad, he wouldn't have thrown me."

Kaylee thought that because she had disagreed with her husband and made him mad, she was just as bad as he was for breaking her thumb. She was trying to assert her contribution to the family, but she broke the rules against disagreeing and seeing the "facts" differently than the BP/NP and by pushing the BP/NP to acknowledge their different views. Trying to get acknowledgment for her contribution infuriated her narcissist husband. She quickly went back to the insane thinking of being just alike to make peace in the family. It is not surprising that Caretakers get very confused about the similarities and differences in individuals.

You may begin to think that you are just as impaired as the BP/NP spouse or parent. Most books and articles about marriage emphasize that both people in the relationship are equally responsible for how the relationship works. To you this can be translated into, "My partner and I are just alike." Yes, you do your share to keep this impaired relationships going, but *what* you do is often very small or even the *opposite* of what the BP/NP does. Consider these examples:

> You take one drink of alcohol and then see yourself the "same" as your alcoholic spouse.
> The BP/NP complains that you are selfish when you want to do something in a different way, so you always do it his or her way.
> The BP/NP screams obscenities at you for three hours. When you finally get mad and yell back one comment, you see yourself as "just like" the BP/NP.
> You constantly think of the needs of the BP/NP and are shocked and confused when the BP/NP sees you as controlling.

Without the ability to see yourself as a separate and unique individual with your own thoughts, feelings, needs, and so on, you will remain in a fog of continuously shifting realities. Changing your ideas about what is real, what is right, what is loyal, and what is proper is a monumental task. But the fact that Caretakers love logic so much is a big help to you in making these adjustments. When you look closely, you will see that many of the thoughts and beliefs you were taught about relationships, especially with the BP/NP, are just plain illogical. Start questioning your way of thinking about your relationship with the BP/NP. If relationships at work and with your friends are pleasant, effective, and enjoyable, why is the relationship with the BP/NP so disturbing and painful? There must be a reason for the difference. The difference is that you think and act differently at work than you do around the BP/NP. Bringing logic into your own observations and beliefs about relationships could help you act more honestly and congruently at home. This change would increase your self-esteem and sense of identify and start moving you out of the Caretaker role.

Chapter Seven

Behavioral Distortions of Caretakers

Caretakers continuously change their behaviors to accommodate what the BP/NP needs from moment to moment. Your behaviors become contingent on what the BP/NP is doing, thinking, feeling, and wanting. You try to "handle" the chaos. You try to please the BP/NP. You try to make life calmer and more predictable. You may get so used to plans falling through because of the BP/NP's sabotage, inability to function, or suddenly changing emotions at the last moment that you give up planning anything you want. What's the use of making plans of your own when the BP/NP's drama could cancel everything? You may find yourself giving up more and more easily. Eventually, you find that you cannot identify what you like or want to do anymore. Your life revolves around the BP/NP's likes and wants.

CHAOS IS PERFECTLY NORMAL: DENIAL

Chaos is a constant in the relationship dominated by a BP/NP. Because BP/NPs react strongly and emotionally to even minor mishaps, misunderstandings, or disappointments, there is always some emotionally charged event happening. This is why *denial* is used so much in BP/NP families. The fastest way to get out of chaos, especially when normal problem solving is not an option, is to forget about what just happened and move on as quickly as possible. Denial is a defense mechanism that even young children can use.

> When we got to the restaurant, John was already very tense. The kids hadn't been ready when John wanted to leave, the car was low on gas, and John was already griping about how much it was going to cost. When our table wasn't ready as soon as we got there, John started telling the hostess she was incompetent, and he loudly demanded to be seated immediately. Then when one of the kids began whining, he looked around with a hostile stare and told her to

shut up. We got seated pretty quickly, and, thankfully, John went into withdrawal mode. I tried to be cheerful and talk with the kids about how much fun
we were having going out to eat. After a while, we all kind of forgot the upset
about getting seated and just tried to have a good time. (Janet, 34, two children
and BP husband)

Caretakers feel their main job is to keep the family atmosphere from deteriorating into chaos, hostility, and hurt feelings. It becomes your job to anticipate the needs of the BP/NP as well as of the children. Many Caretakers
describe life with a BP/NP as having another kid in an adult body to take care
of.

As a Caretaker, you are certainly good at putting on a happy face, acting
calm, and smoothing things over. Denial of the confusion and chaos and
acting as if everything is fine may feel like second nature. You tolerate an
amazing amount of emotional chaos before even noticing that anything is
amiss. Behaviors that would drive a noncaretaker away quickly from a relationship often don't even register with you. You may even be proud of
yourself for how well you do in a crisis. This keeps you from recognizing
that chaos really isn't normal.

How would your life feel without all that chaos? If you didn't have to
devote your full attention to the BP/NP, there would be more time to be self-
conscious and perhaps feel vulnerable. When the attention of the interaction
isn't always on the BP/NP but actually comes to rest on you at times, does it
leave you unsure about how to act? You may find that it is really uncomfortable and not know what you want to do. Being the focus of attention and
having your needs considered may be something you have always wanted
but have little experience with. You may find it surprisingly uncomfortable.
So without the chaos, normal may not feel so normal.

I CAN'T MAKE SENSE OF IT ALL: MYSTIFICATION

When you try to smooth things over by pretending that nothing strange is
happening in your relationship with the BP/NP, you create a disturbing lie to
yourself and everyone else about your life. Even when things look relatively
calm on the surface, the underlying feelings in the relationship are uncertainty, anxiety, distrust, and not knowing what is actually happening or what will
happen next. This creates great anxiety in children and in you as well. Do
you notice that you are always waiting for the next disaster?

Pretending that things are okay when they are not is called mystification.
It creates more chaos and confusion in the relationship. Pretending that you
are happy when you're angry or pretending that you are in agreement when
you are not starts making your life and relationship a fantasy rather than
reality. Mystification can lead to a lot of misunderstandings, poor communi-

cation, wrong conclusions, and disappointed expectations in a relationship that is already difficult to negotiate as it is.

The greatest mystification that Caretakers do is the lie you tell yourself that everything is okay in the relationship. How much energy and time are you spending covering up the reality that you are in a relationship with a mentally ill person, all the while pretending that your partner is "normal" and that your drama-laced interactions are "normal"? The fantasy that the BP/NP is just like everybody else, only "more intense," is a mystification. What do you tell your friends and family about the BP/NP's odd or rude or hysterical behavior? The person you mystify the most is yourself.

HYPERVIGILANCE

It doesn't take long for Caretakers to develop a strong reaction of hypervigilance when in a relationship with a BP/NP. This means that you are always on the alert, watching the BP/NP for any nuance of change in mood or feeling because these can be so quick and volatile from one extreme to another. As a Caretaker, you may think that your job to soothe and calm the BP/NP will be easier if you anticipate and head off negative and explosive reactions. This leads many Caretakers to have an uncanny, almost seemingly psychic ability to read body language, interpret even minute changes in facial expressions, and be able to anticipate trouble in the making. Hypervigilance can be exhausting and can lead to an increase in feelings of trepidation, anxiety, and even a sense of doom. It is essentially being on high danger alert all the time. It takes a toll.

ISOLATING

Over time, Caretakers often become more and more isolating. Although you may normally enjoy socializing, you may start to fear social situations that include the BP/NP.

> I used to socialize a lot with my friends and family until I met Chuck. He is always so jealous and calls me 10 to 15 times when I am at lunch with my girlfriends or if I stop by to see my nieces and nephews after work. He is always suspicious and checking up on me. He "forbade" me to go to my college reunion because he was sure I would have an affair. I even quit getting my weekly massage because he accused me of meeting an old boyfriend. Whenever I suggest we go to dinner at my parents, he has a fit or refuses to go at the last minute. He never likes anyone that I like. It's just takes so much energy to deal with all the third degree. My friends and family all think that I just don't care about them anymore because I make so many excuses and

cancel at the last minute. I feel like I can't pay attention to anyone else except
Chuck or his feelings get hurt. (Marie, age 37, NP boyfriend)

Caretakers find that it is very chancy to count on a BP/NP in a social situation. Even creating a special evening at home or just as a couple can lead to
surprising anxiety and anger from the BP.

> I set up a great evening for our anniversary. I made reservations at Janet's
> favorite restaurant, hired a limousine, had champagne, everything. I was going
> to surprise her with a special evening. But she found out about the plans and
> literally refused to go. She was worried about the cost, and she didn't want to
> leave the kids for the evening, and she said she didn't have a nice dress. I told
> her that I had all that taken care of, but she still refused to budge. We spent the
> evening in different rooms. It was then that I decided I needed to get a social
> life of my own. (David, 32, BP wife)

Social anxiety is a huge issue for many BP/NPs unless they can be in control
of the situation. For example, they may be willing to go only if they can be
the center of attention or decide everything that is going to happen. As a
result, you may give up making social plans from frustration, disappointment, or just embarrassment. You just become less and less social.

In addition, many BP/NPs seek to isolate the Caretaker from either one or
both families and even from your friends. One borderline husband told his
wife not to talk to his mother about anything that she hadn't cleared with him
beforehand. A narcissist wife refused to spend time with her husband's family because they were too boring and uncouth, and she put him down with
insults every time he tried to visit them on his own. She felt he was abandoning her if he visited his parents without her. He finally gave up.

BP/NPs feel a strong sense of abandonment whenever you want to do
anything without them. Their insecurities can take so much energy to manage
that it can become not worth it to fight for two hours about a 10-minute call
to a friend. So over time, you may find yourself giving up on friendships and
social events. The BP/NP wants to be the sole focus of your energy. Even
managing the needs of the children can become secondary to meeting the BP/
NP's needs. Have you ever just dropped into bed at night exhausted and
wondering, Is this all there is?

However, the more isolated you become and the more you lose track of
your own needs and interests, the more you get pulled into the delusional
thinking of the BP/NP and then the less able you will be to make sense of
what is happening. Without social support or an outside frame of reference
like friends or family, you can end up feeling stuck in a nightmare of confusion that seems impossible to get out of. You may even feel embarrassed to
discuss what is going on in your relationship even on a casual basis with
friends. If you do try to describe the truth of your relationship to a friend or

relative, the gravity and level of dysfunction is rarely understood by the listener. This can end up making you feel even more isolated and lost.

THE BP/NP ALWAYS GETS TO DECIDE

When couples believe that they must do everything together, the one who says "No" always determines what happens. However, the relationship between a BP/NP and the Caretaker is based on the premise that it is against the rules for the Caretaker to say "No." Have you noticed that when you attempt to say "No," the BP/NP emotionally erupts, withdraws, pouts, or attacks? It is the Caretaker's responsibility to do whatever the BP/NP decides. Rarely will the BP/NP do what you want just because you want to do it. And since there is such a strong expectation in the relationship that you do everything together, eventually this, too, discourages you from doing the things you want to do.

MANIPULATION

It is very likely you see the BP/NP as a master manipulator. It may be hard to see what a master manipulator you, too, have become trying to "handle" this relationship. If there is no way to get what you want from a direct approach, then manipulation is the only solution. Manipulation is the tool of the powerless person. You feel powerless. It may surprise you to know that the BP/NP also feels powerless. This relationship is full of maneuvering and manipulation.

To function in any effective way in your relationship with the BP/NP, you have learned to manipulate situations, too. You may find that it takes a lot of special tactics to create results that will be workable for you, the children, and the BP/NP. One Caretaker said she wanted to invite her husband's family over for Thanksgiving and asked her husband about two months ahead of time. The husband said it was too late, that he needed a year to get ready for such an event. The Caretaker spent the next year easing her husband into the possibility of a Thanksgiving together as an extended family by talking another relative into hosting the event. She was elated that her husband consented to go. This gives a picture of the amount of energy and thought that often must go into these kinds of changes for the BP/NP. If you're been in the relationship with a BP/NP for some time, you may have found a way through manipulation to get him or her to think that everything is his or her idea.

Manipulation can be done for good or ill. Good manipulation serves the needs of everyone without hurting anyone else. Bad manipulation hurts others. However, it is not easy to stay on the side of good when one begins to manipulate on a regular basis. No one is completely and consistently unself-ish in this process. So when you become angry and frustrated and go through bouts of needing to change things, you may start thinking of ways to do it with negative manipulation. Turning to passive-aggressive behaviors, trick-ery, name-calling, put-downs, and even violence are all means of trying to change the power differential in relationships when it feels impossible to get results from being direct and reasonable. You may have to watch yourself very carefully, or you could find yourself doing some of the same negative manipulations that you see in your BP/NP partner. It may fill a need for revenge, but it is never effective when done for meanness, payback, or just plain anger.

Being caught in manipulative interactions for too long may lead you to believe there is no other way to get what you want. Caretakers raised by BP/NPs are the most vulnerable to being unwilling or unable to use more direct means to get needs met. You've had a lifetime of training in manipulation. Even though you know how to be effective and assertive and to ask directly for what you want at work, at school, or with friends, you may find it difficult to do the same in a BP/NP relationship. You may have never learned any other means to deal with differences and wants in this highly intense and sometimes volatile relationship.

You may be, understandably, wary of changing the system of manipula-tion that you have established to make things work in your relationship with the BP/NP. You could be afraid of the BP/NP's anger, power of saying "No," as well as his or her disapproval, withdrawal, or scowls. You may fear abandonment, disruption of a known pattern, and the BP/NP's hostility. This, of course, keeps you enslaved emotionally to meeting the needs of the BP/NP no matter how much this may deny your own needs. Reliance on manipula-tion rather than directness can be a major factor that keeps you in the Care-taker role.

THERE'S NO TIME TO TAKE CARE OF ME

Obviously, if you are caretaking a BP/NP, then it stands to reason that your needs aren't getting taken care of. When I ask Caretakers how they take care of themselves, I usually get blank stares or explanations that they would feel better if the BP/NP would just think of his or her needs. You may think that taking care of the BP/NP actually is taking care of yourself. However, this is a good example of your thinking that you and the BP/NP are fused into one. When only one person's needs get met, they will always be the BP/NP's needs, not yours.

You may be too overwhelmed or exhausted to notice that your needs are not being met. However, when you eventually do notice, you may be shocked and angry to see how little you get. This book may be opening your eyes to how much you are ignoring in your own life. You may want to blame the BP/NP, or you may blame yourself for being so needy. But you are human (not superhuman), and you do have needs.

One of the big problems with taking care of your own needs is that you may never have identified what your needs are. You may have very little idea of what you want other than a vague idea of being happy, feeling loved, or being cared for. If you can't put these general feelings into some concrete behavioral terms, you can't get very far in filling those needs.

WHY SHOULD I HAVE TO TAKE CARE OF MYSELF?

When you share with others that your needs are not being met, you may get told by a friend or a therapist that you could consider meeting your own needs. If you are like many Caretakers, you may find this idea very upsetting. It flies in the face of your deepest fantasy that the BP/NP will eventually love you enough to start considering what you need and want to give it to you. You have spent your life taking care of the BP/NPs needs; when will it ever be your turn? It doesn't feel fair. And it isn't fair.

After all, you have invested all of your energy, time, and love into the BP/NP. Thinking about meeting your own needs on top of all that you do for the BP/NP and your other family members may seem absolutely impossible. Giving up your hope and fantasy of someday having your needs met by the BP/NP may also seem like a terrible defeat. It may mean coming face-to-face with the fear that this relationship cannot be made to work in a give-and-take manner no matter how much you give.

It can be disconcerting to see how many ways your behaviors have been influenced and governed by your relationship with the BP/NP. Perhaps this chapter shows you how much you need to be consciously aware of the things you do and really consider if these behaviors are a good representation of who you are and who you want to be.

WE ARE ONE: LACK OF BOUNDARIES

Enmeshment and lack of boundaries are universal and seemingly necessary elements for the BP/NP's definition of love and caring. Enmeshment results when you and the BP/NP merge into one, and it is exemplified by behaviors such as talking for each other, assuming that both of you think the same about everything, expecting to react or feel exactly the same in a situation, lack of privacy, assuming that everything that belongs to one belongs to the other, and always using "we" instead of "I" (e.g., "we think" and "we feel").

Enmeshment happens to some extent in most long-term relationships, but it is extreme in the relationship with the BP/NP.

Enmeshment becomes oppressive and damaging to your self esteem and identity when you are not allowed to have a different thought, opinion, or feeling. One of the unhealthy results of enmeshment is the right that the BP/NP and you take on yourselves to correct, fix, and demand that the other change to meet your wants and expectations. When requests for change move into demands and commands, the relationship becomes unhealthy for everyone.

Caretakers have the ability to have a separate identity, but you may easily fall into the belief that you must or should be enmeshed to show your love and caring for the BP/NP. Enmeshment can also be the basis of your fear of anger. Anger and disagreement are proof that the two of you aren't feeling and thinking as one, and this makes the BP/NP—and maybe you as well— feel that you don't love each other. So enmeshment serves to bring you back into the Caretaker role to merge and serve the needs of the BP/NP.

Chapter Eight

Distortions in the Sense of Self

Caretakers have a pretty well-defined sense of self (SOS). Before getting into this relationship, you probably knew a lot about yourself and acted consistently. You knew your strengths and weaknesses. Your values and morals were established. You saw yourself pretty much the same way your friends and family described you. Usually, you have been described as caring, conscientious, friendly, considerate, and giving. You may not be so sure of who you are after being in a long-term relationship with the BP/NP. The BP/NP's description of you can vary wildly, but more often than not, he or she sees you as selfish, thoughtless, mean, and wrong.

These two very different pictures of *you* from family and friends versus from the BP/NP become very confusing. Caretakers like to be "good" people. You especially like to please the person you love and find it easy to believe their complaints about you. If the BP/NP says that you're selfish, you will probably try your hardest to be giving, kind, and even overly considerate to change the BP/NP's view of you to match what you believe about yourself. If the BP/NP says that you are mean, you will more than likely give in to whatever he or she wants in order to show that you are caring. You begin to exaggerate your kindly behaviors at the same time that you start doubting your perceptions of who you are. However, this giving in and giving up only seems to reinforce the accusations from the BP/NP and increases your own self-doubts.

Your SOS becomes more fragile around the BP/NP, and you may often feel a need to try to get the BP/NP to see you more as you see yourself. However, the emotional and logical distortions of the BP/NP can lead to a skewed picture of who you are, one that isn't likely to change. You may become frustrated and angry at the BP/NP's insistence that you are uncaring and selfish, yet at the same time you doubt your own perceptions more and more.

SOS AS AN ARENA OF CONFLICT

The SOS is a primary arena of conflict in Caretaker/BP/NP relationships, even though this may not seem obvious at first. The conflict is over whose SOS, that is, whose ideas, feelings, thoughts, and beliefs will be the prevailing ones in the relationship. In order to feel comfortable, the BP/NP needs you to feel, think, act, and believe exactly as he or she does. The BP/NP demands that you conform to his or her definition of the SOS that is the "right" one, that is, theirs.

You may try for a while to match the BP/NP's SOS, but that just leads to you feeling devalued, invisible, and not seen or considered. Eventually, your SOS will shrivel and go underground, or you will have to find a way to be seen and heard by the BP/NP. But every time you disagree, have a different feeling, or want to do something the BP/NP doesn't want, you are considered selfish, disloyal, uncaring, and unloving. You end up fighting for your point of view, and the BP/NP fights for his or hers. The whole premise that there can and should be only one SOS is the distortion.

FUZZY AND SHIFTING SOS

Your SOS usually works well in nonintimate interactions. You have developed a constant, internal picture of yourself that works effectively on the job, in social situations, and even with most friends. In those situations, you can clearly identify your values, goals, needs, and wants in practical, concrete terms. However, in the relationship with the BP/NP, you find yourself using vague, emotional descriptions of what you want and who you are, such as "I just want to be happy" or "I'm a caring person." You may also find yourself lured away from your own values or SOS to please or accommodate the BP/NP whom you love. Listen to Marion:

> My husband [an NP] was having an affair with one of my friends. I was terribly upset by that. However, in a discussion on limiting his contact with her, we ended up with me actually giving him more time with her. How did that happen? I really don't know. In fact, looking back, I am stunned that we were even having a discussion about limits on his time with her instead of discussing his ending the affair or I was leaving. I remember being petrified that if he left, I wouldn't be able to function on my own.

Marion is a physician and holds a highly responsible position in a hospital, but her caretaking at home led her into a lot of poor decisions and unhappy situations with her husband. Although she has good self-esteem at work, her experiences with a belittling, narcissistic mother and a rejecting narcissistic husband have left her feeling personally unlovable, undeserving, and fearful of being on her own. She keeps trying to please her mother and husband in hopes that they will finally accept her. She finds it hard to get a handle on pleasing herself and doing what she knows is right for her own well-being when her mother and/or husband disagree with her.

You may find yourself more confused about who you are the longer you stay with the NP/BP. How you see yourself is so different from how your NP/BP partner sees you and may be very much at odds with how you act around him or her that you begin to feel more and more confused yourself.

HIDDEN NEGATIVE SOS

You may be extremely aware of the negativity in the borderline's SOS. And you may be able to see the hidden criticism and negative expectations in the narcissist. But you may not see to what extent you, too, may also be carrying a negative SOS.

Caretakers typically think of themselves as strong, positive, caring, and healthy, and much of the time you are. However, Caretakers too often carry an internal negative self-esteem and self-attitude that is often hidden, maybe even from yourself. This negative SOS exists right under the positive SOS. It is composed of myriad negative messages that you have "taken to heart" and internalized, usually as the result of words, attitudes, and comments from the NP/BP parent or spouse. The constant demand for perfection in yourself, your need to seek approval from the BP/NP, and your failure to "fix" the borderline, to get the narcissist to love you, or to somehow make everyone's life happy may make you feel that you are a failure and to blame for the all the problems in this relationship.

This wearing down and giving up of your positive SOS leads to hopelessness, a feeling of being overwhelmed, and chronic depression. Over time, you lose the positive-thinking, upbeat person you used to be.

BEING A CARETAKER MEANS I'M A GOOD PERSON

Although you see yourself as "being a good person," inside you may feel deeply unworthy, unloved, and damaged. You may wonder why it has been your lot that you care for someone else rather than being cared for. Do you ever wonder why is it that you are required to meet such high demands? It can seem impossible to believe that you have had a part in putting these expectations on yourself, and it may take you a while to release yourself from the slavery of being the Caretaker for the BP/NP.

Not seeing yourself as the strong, loving, good Caretaker may leave you with a deficit in your SOS. If you aren't constantly in the Caretaker role, does that mean that you are uncaring, heartless, mean, and selfish, in other words, everything you have been told you are by the BP/NP when you aren't doing what he or she wants? Many Caretakers literally refuse to face these horrible feelings even to get themselves into a happier life. They absolutely believe that it is impossible to be a good person and not be a Caretaker. Do you?

BEING CARING *OF* VERSUS CARING *FOR*

The difference between caring *for* others and being caring *of* others is that when you care *for* others, you are doing for them what they should be doing for themselves. In families, we appropriately care *for* children, but we should be caring *of* other adults. When you are caring *of* others, you give them the respect and freedom to be who they are, to take care of themselves, and to be responsible for their own actions.

Caring *for* the BP/NP may seem essential to making your relationship and family work. It includes giving in to the emotional coercion of the BP/NP, keeping the peace by giving up what you want, and blaming the BP/NP for "making" you do things all because it quiets the BP/NP's moods and behaviors. It means hiding your feelings to make the BP/NP think you are in agreement, making excuses for the BP/NP's behavior, and giving up who you know yourself to be.

Clinging to the role of Caretaker really means giving up caring for yourself and, instead, focusing all your energy on taking care of the BP/NP for fear that you could be overwhelmed, annihilated, or abandoned if you don't.

Being caring *of* the BP/NP would mean allowing the BP/NP to be just who he or she is. It would include caring that the BP/NP is angry, hurt, fearful, and demanding without feeling responsible to "make" him or her feel better, without feeling that you "caused" the problem, and without thinking that you have to fix his or her feelings or do what the BP/NP wants.

Being caring *of* the BP/NP would mean staying emotionally detached from his or her mental and emotional distortions. Of course, the only way to make that work would be for you to be truly who you are and then see what this relationship is really about.

The idea of being caring *of* the BP/NP may seem impossible to you and maybe even dangerous. You may find it hard to imagine how taking care of yourself and letting the BP/NP take care of him- or herself will make life better. You may discover that you don't know how to be if you are not a Caretaker and have no idea of any other possible way to function. Later chapters will provide many helpful steps and ideas about what to do instead.

Chapter Nine

Relationship Distortions of Caretakers

If you have distortions in your emotions, thoughts, behaviors, and sense of self, you will have distortions in your ideas about relationships. There are many imbalances in Caretaker/BP/NP relationships. Some of the most prominent distortions that Caretakers have about the relationship with the BP/NP include the beliefs that the BP/NP is the problem so that you shouldn't have to change, fear of disagreement and anger, keeping secrets to protect the relationship, trying to fix the past, reversal of adult/child roles in the family, and the victim/rescuer/persecutor pattern.

WHY AM I THE ONE WHO HAS TO CHANGE?

You probably, rightly, believe that you have already made a monumental number of changes to accommodate your relationship with the BP/NP. You can see that the BP/NP is functioning poorly, and you likely believe that the solution is to get the BP/NP to change and become more reasonable, logical, and emotionally healthy. However, the overwhelming problem is that the BP/NP is either unwilling or unable to make changes. That is part of the difficulty with personality disorders: people who have them cannot perceive the changes needed, they feel threatened by change, and they often don't follow through with the changes needed.

In addition, focusing on changing another person keeps you from figuring out how the relationship works from *your* perspective and learning to change things in yourself. So, if you want the relationship with the BP/NP to be different, you must be the one to make the changes. Think about it. Haven't you tried over and over to change the BP/NP and seen little or no change?

Perhaps you have thought that your failure was due to something you were doing wrong. The real truth is that *you can't force the BP/NP to change.*

73

In fact, you can't force *anyone* else to change. No one has the power to make anyone else change. Each of us has the power to change only ourselves. You have been looking for a way to have more power in this relationship, and this is the key. You have been focusing in the wrong place.

It is not that the BP/NP is taking your self-esteem away; it is you who is volunteering to give up on your own needs, wants, and values by constantly focusing all of your energy on the BP/NP. Get over wanting to change the BP/NP, quit trying to change the BP/NP, and start focusing on what you actually have the power to change, that is, yourself.

FEAR OF ANGER

Caretakers most often say that they give in and give up and do everything that the BP/NP wants primarily to avoid the BP/NP's anger. Yes, the BP/NP does use anger as a way to control others. But why are you so sensitive to his or her anger? Does your reaction to the BP/NP's anger feel like knives going through you, being annihilated, or falling off a cliff? These are descriptions I have heard from Caretakers in my practice. Having an extremely fearful reaction to anger really gets in your way of having a healthy, effective relationship, and it leaves you vulnerable to being manipulated and blackmailed by that anger.

Learning to stand your ground in disagreements and to handle the BP/NP's anger is essential for you to function without being so vulnerable. Your fear of the BP/NP's anger leads you to actually reinforce and increase this pattern of emotional blackmail from the BP/NP every time you give in to his or her demands when the BP/NP is angry.

What makes you so afraid of the BP/NP's anger? Are you also that afraid of anger in other people? If not, why not? Why can't you tolerate the BP/NP's being angry for a few hours or even days? Why do you become so miserable when the BP/NP is angry? What fears come to the surface? Do you know how to calm your anxiety when the BP/NP is angry? Are you actually in danger when the BP/NP is angry?

Becoming mindful of what your fears are really about when the BP/NP is angry can lead you to changing your relationship with the BP/NP in significant ways. Being easily manipulated by anger means that you are giving up your power in the relationship.

KEEPING IT ALL SECRET

Caretakers are especially prone to keeping the difficult and upsetting interactions with their BP/NP partner a secret so that you and the relationship will look good to the rest of the world. Not only are you hiding the truth about your relationship from the rest of the world, but you may also be hiding this truth from yourself. Part of how you keep yourself in the Caretaker role is by keeping a fantasy image of your relationship—what you wish it were rather than looking at it as it really is.

If you are very good at ignoring, repressing, and hiding the reality of your relationship with the NP/BP, you will get very little helpful support or reality checks from your family and friends. Keeping your relationship workings a secret allows the BP/NP to keep the status quo and keep control of you. Do you actively avoid letting others see the internal dysfunction in your relationship because you don't want to face the reality of your problems? If you want things to change and you want more support in your life, you will need to stop keeping secrets from yourself and others, be more honest, and reach out to get that support.

TRYING TO FIX THE PAST

Although Freud said that people select a marriage partner who is like the parent of the opposite gender, a more updated selection process has been observed. People coming from dysfunctional families select a marriage partner who is most like the significant family member with whom they have "unfinished business."[1] That means that if you had a BP/NP parent, grandparent, or sibling, you are much more vulnerable to selecting a BP/NP spouse. And if you learned the Caretaker role in your family because of a BP/NP member, you will more easily take on the Caretaker role in your adult relationships. You are more willing to put up with relationships that are not equal, to give up your needs for others, and to expect more adult and responsible behavior from yourself than from others when you have learned these patterns growing up.

What is unfinished business? This refers to intimate interactions, emotions, beliefs, and patterned behaviors that you developed in childhood that you continue to follow with the BP/NP in the present even when you see that they don't work. When you couldn't solve the childhood relationship problems with a BP/NP or other dysfunctional parent, you became vulnerable to seeking adult relationships where you could continue to try to solve the same problems. Some examples follow:

If you didn't feel understood by your parent, you may pick a partner who also fails to understand you.

If you were too frequently criticized by a parent or sibling, you may pick a partner who also criticizes you.

If you felt rejected by your parent, you may pick a spouse who is also rejecting of you.

If you didn't get adequate emotional reassurance from your parent, you
may pick a partner who is unsupportive.

If you were held responsible for a dysfunctional sibling's behavior, you
may easily feel responsible for you current partner's BP/NP behavior.

When you first fell in love with your current BP/NP partner, he or she may
have looked and acted quite different from your prior BP/NP or dysfunctional family member, but as the relationship got more intimate, you may have
discovered that your partner was actually more similar than you realized.
This pattern of unfinished business or repeated patterns in marriage relationships has been observed for decades in the issues of alcoholism, multiple
divorces, early pregnancies, abuse, and high conflict as well. Your family of
origin is your template for how you live in relationships now unless you
work to consciously change it.

REVERSAL OF ADULT/CHILD ROLES

By colluding with the BP/NP, you are actually supporting the reversal of
rules and roles in the family between the BP/NP adult and the children. You
are asking your children to act more maturely than the adult BP/NP. You ask
the children to follow rules, do chores, and act civil but don't expect the same
of the BP/NP for fear of causing an argument. The children get confused and
angry when they see the BP/NP constantly breaking these family rules and
expectations with no comment by you. Of course, you are in a terrible double
bind. You cannot make the BP/NP act any differently, whereas you can,
probably, get the children to act more adultlike. So you do what you can. But
this reversal confuses your children's ability to see reality clearly and leads
them into unfinished business of their own.

VICTIM/PERSECUTOR/RESCUER PATTERN

One of the most repeated patterns in dysfunctional relationships is falling
into the victim/persecutor/rescuer pattern described in chapter 2. Caretakers
often like to see themselves as the "good" person. This translates into being
the rescuer. Trying to fix, soothe, placate, care for, and appease the BP/NP
are all forms of rescuing. As long as you play any of these three roles in this
pattern, you will find yourself stuck being a Caretaker. The pattern is never
healthy in families, it never fixes anything, and it retards the growth of all
family members.

The distortions in your own emotions, thinking, behaviors, identity, and
relationships work together to keep you trapped in the Caretaker role with the
BP/NP. You have participated in creating patterns in this relationship that

work against your being fully and truly who you could be. You keep yourself from knowing who you are, being aware of what you want, and leading the life that you truly would like based on these distortions and your inner fears. The likelihood of the BP/NP's changing any of his or her distortions is negligible. But you have the ability to see reality, and you have the skills to change how you function. Do you have the courage to make changes to these distortions that you have been using so that you can reclaim your true sense of self and make your unique contribution to your life and the lives of others?

II

Letting Go of Caretaking

INTRODUCTION: HOW DO I MAKE CHANGES?

How do you change the distortions that you have been using? How do you change the patterns of colluding with the BP/NP that have tricked you into giving up your own beliefs, goals, and desires for your life? How do you change the antagonism, powerlessness, and anger you feel when interacting with the BP/NP into a sense of self-confidence and powerfulness over your own life? How do you stop caretaking the BP/NP and get a life of your own?

It will require you to make large changes in your thinking, your language, and your basic way of doing things. It is both harder than you can imagine and easier than you can believe. Don't be surprised if you feel angry, relieved, disbelieving, overjoyed, and scared as you embark on this new life change process.

It is important here to point out that recovery from being a Caretaker cannot be done alone. It is not a "pull yourself up by your bootstraps" kind of plan. If you grew up with a close BP/NP family member, you may have some very long-term, dysfunctional relationship patterns that come up automatically in stressful situations, especially with other BP/NPs. Changing basic core beliefs, outlined in earlier chapters, is extremely difficult or impossible to do alone.

It is really important to get help from others. In order to learn how healthy relationships work, you need models and directions. It is also wonderful to have healthy people around to help you practice new behaviors and to give you encouragement and support. Look around for the healthy people and relationships in your life that you already have, such as coworkers, other family members, and friends. In addition, you may want to search out a knowledgeable therapist who has had experience working with borderline and narcissistic personality disorders. Both individual and group therapy that is specifically focused on Caretaker recovery can help you move toward your goals more quickly.

Chapter Ten

Stages of Healing

Years ago when I read about Elizabeth Kubler-Ross's stages of dying, it seemed clear to me that her stages represented a universal process of letting go and moving forward from loss toward health and renewal. I felt that her stages could apply to nearly any major transition that we go through in life, and I believe that they apply very well to the process of healing from being a Caretaker. I have added three additional stages that describe the further steps that are needed to specifically move forward out of the Caretaker role and into the stage of self-care.

DENIAL

Denial is the stage of status quo and the beginning awareness of feeling that something isn't right, but, at the same time, you don't want to really look at it. Perhaps that is where you were when you picked up this book. You may have had a sense that life was very upsetting, but you couldn't put your finger on what was wrong. You may have had a sense that the BP/NP in your life is not normal, but an encompassing cloud of doubt and uncertainty keeps you wondering whether it is really you who is "crazy." You may also find it impossible to imagine what and how things can change because you have tried, perhaps for years, to change the BP/NP with little success. Conversely, you may get caught up in the mystification of seeing only the good and the positive possibilities when the BP/NP is acting "normal" and "nice" with the hope that he or she really understands and is going to change. These thoughts and feelings are all part of the stage of denial.

Your hope that the BP/NP will finally see and hear *you* and respond to *your* needs or your belief that the BP/NP will finally understand how to be caring and sharing are hopes and beliefs that are strongly motivating. Your deep need for the BP/NP see what his or her behavior is doing to you and to make the changes that could heal your relationship are all part of denial.

Denial keeps you from doing what you could actually do to change your life in the positive direction you would really like to go. As long as you keep hoping, believing, and needing the BP/NP to be different rather than taking the steps that *you* could take to make things different, you are in the stage of denial.

Denial is a stage of nonmovement. It is a place of not wanting to look at the full truth of what is actually happening in your life, not wanting to recognize the difficult steps that actually need to be taken. Years ago, I heard the saying, "Confusion is the mind's way of buying time." Living with a BP/NP is definitely confusing, but staying in that confusion is a form of denial. In the denial stage, you are buying time for things to *somehow* get better without disrupting your life and without your having to really make the big changes that might end a relationship, create chaos, make someone angry, or initiate rejection.

The capacity of Caretakers to hang out in the stage of denial, sometimes for years or decades, is astounding to friends and family. Most people find the sheer anxiety of being on edge with the confusion and uproar that you live with nearly intolerable. Yet you may be so much in denial and so used to this state of being that moving out of it can feel very frightening.

It may be surprising to find out that whenever you push for the BP/NP to make the changes needed to create a life for you as the Caretaker to feel better, you are keeping yourself in denial. Over and over, Caretakers focus on the changes that the BP/NP "should" make, such as being more appreciative, criticizing less, not getting angry so easily, being more cooperative, doing his or her fair share, and so on. These may seem like reasonable changes to ask for, but what you are in denial about is that the BP/NP *cannot or won't make these changes*. What you are deeply in denial about is that it will have to be *you*, the Caretaker, who has to make all the changes if your life is to be different.

You may think that you have already made an incredible number of changes just to accommodate the BP/NP, and that is true. You have probably changed how you say things, the words you use, or your inflection, or you have put all your attention and energy on caring for the fragile emotions of the BP/NP, or have been amazingly flexible in adjusting to the BP/NP's changing moods and needs, and so on. And you are right. You have made all those kinds of changes, but those changes don't really change the core dysfunctions in your relationship with the BP/NP. You haven't changed the relationship, nor have you changed the patterns that control how you interact in the relationship.

Those changes have simply made it possible for you to accommodate the BP/NP but have not made a better relationship for you or for the BP/NP.

Those changes may actually have reinforced the dysfunctional behaviors of the BP/NP, and they have probably worn you to a frazzle.

Real changes would have to include thinking differently about yourself and the world, setting limits on how the BP/NP treats you, and coming to terms with the reality of the ongoing mental illness in the BP/NP. Instead of just hoping for the best and reacting to what the BP/NP does, real change requires you to invest in a whole new system of thinking, believing, and acting. This kind of change requires much greater time, greater resources, and greater courage than you have put in so far. Therefore, denial can seem much more preferable. But by picking up this book, going to therapy, or getting to the "end of your rope," the stage of denial begins to be challenged.

ANGER

The stage of anger usually occurs as the result of being prodded out of the familiar stage of "denial." Anger typically cycles in and out along with denial. Anger comes up most often when the BP/NP is acting "crazy," hostile, hurtful, selfish, illogical, and so on, alternating with denial when the BP/NP is behaving more normally. Caretakers don't usually like being angry, so the anger stage can get pushed back into denial rather quickly much of the time.

The stage of anger is often felt at first by Caretakers as hurt, frustration, shock, disbelief, and confusion. So, initially, anger is combined with a lot of denial. Your feelings of anger come about from having expectations that the BP/NP would, should, or could act normally. There is not yet an acknowledgment that the BP/NP has a real and permanent mental disorder. Anger also occurs because you believe that you could or should be able to "fix" the BP/NP and that if the BP/NP loved you more, the BP/NP could and should act more loving and positive. These beliefs end up creating feelings of incompetence and being unloved, again bringing up anger.

You may begin to believe that if the BP/NP could just understand the level of upset about his or her behavior toward you, then he or she would stop acting badly and everything would be fine. So Caretakers sometimes feel that they must convey to the BP/NP the level of their distress as a means to get the BP/NP to be more loving and considerate. You may get so frustrated that you explode in anger at the BP/NP. However, this won't be successful in making anything change. Acting out your anger in this relationship is forbidden, so the BP/NP reacts with more rage and you feel ashamed and hurt. You end up still feeling angry, but now you begin stuffing it. This results in your building more and more resentment and hurt.

The positive thing about being in the stage of anger is that you are beginning to admit that there is a problem and that you are not happy about it. This is an important step in awareness because until you can come to see clearly that you don't like how the relationship is working, nothing can be done to change it. Anger is the first sign of your admitting that the BP/NP is treating you badly and that you don't like it. You are starting to feel that the relationship with the BP/NP is unfair to you and that it really doesn't fit what you want in an intimate relationship.

As you move more fully into the stage of anger, you may become aware of the anger you have at yourself. Your self-anger can alternate with your anger at the BP/NP by going from blaming yourself for not being loving enough to blaming the BP/NP for not being more normal. You may be angry at yourself for picking the BP/NP in the first place. And most Caretakers become angry at themselves for not being able to change the BP/NP.

The stage of anger is a step toward awareness of what is really going on in your relationship with the BP/NP. You feel and see the unfairness as well as the hurt and hostility that are all part of this relationship, and you are becoming aware that you no longer want it to be that way. But truly changing this relationship seems significantly overwhelming, unclear, difficult, and maybe impossible. When you are already using up all of your energy just to cope with things as they are, it can seem too much to deal with actually making significant life changes. Besides, at this stage, you are still thinking that the changes will logically have to be made by the BP/NP, which of course is not going to happen, adding to your anger.

BARGAINING

Bargaining is the stage of no longer being in complete denial but not really being ready to make a lot of big changes. Examples of bargaining that I have seen Caretakers try include going on vacation to make the relationship better, getting a job to take one's mind off of the relationship, initiating a temporary separation, having an affair, having another child, going to couple's therapy to help the BP/NP really understand and change, threatening divorce if things don't change, taking up an addiction (spending, drinking, or eating), buying a new house, starting a business, nagging, withdrawing, or exhibiting continuous hostility.

In the stage of bargaining, you are still trying to make small changes (although these *look* a lot bigger). Yes, you are making changes in what you are doing. However, the reality is that bargaining changes still don't really change the patterns and core of the relationship. They are temporary fixes that mostly take your attention away from the anger and pain that you were beginning to really feel. When the same issues keep popping up after your "changes," it is a sure sign of bargaining rather than real change.

Real change involves dealing with the issue that is at the core of this relationship, especially the fact that the BP/NP has a mental illness. Humans try to bargain away physical illness and even death, so it is not surprising that we would try to bargain away mental illness, which is much less concrete and more confusing. So Caretakers think, If only I could be more loving, if I pray more, if I could make him understand, if she would only think before she speaks, if I take my mind off of the problems, then things would be better. This is all bargaining.

It is very hard not to get involved in bargaining because you love (or have loved) the BP/NP, you've made a long-term investment in the relationship, you may be raising children, have a mortgage, and have a life plan that includes the BP/NP. Since the BP/NP can often look perfectly normal to outsiders, you have also probably been given a lot of advice about how to make things work from well-meaning friends, relatives, ministers, therapists, and so on. This advice encourages you to keep hoping and trying, that is, bargaining rather than facing the difficult and true fact that the BP/NP is seriously mentally ill and that you will need much bigger changes than you have been putting in place.

Denial, anger, and bargaining tend to come in cycles. See figure 10.1 at the end of this chapter. Anger comes when negative events break through your denial. But since anger is so uncomfortable to Caretakers, you move to bargaining to try to change things without rocking the boat too much. Bargaining solutions may work for a few days or months, so then you might even move back into denial that anything is really wrong, until the cycle starts all over when the BP/NP's negative behaviors pop up again.

Sometimes these three stages cycle around for years or decades with little or no progress. Fueled by your own hope and the advice and good intentions of friends and relatives, along with the subsequent periods of bargaining solutions, Caretakers can keep the cycle turning for a long time. The longer the cycle continues, the harder it often is to extricate yourself from it because you think you will lose all of the investment and energy you have put into the bargaining solutions.

Often it is the effect of your relationship with the BP/NP on your children that finally gets you to take a serious look at the failure that is occurring. When your children start having problems functioning at school or making friends or they become depressed or start acting out at home and maybe even in public, the seriousness of the core issues really hits home. Or it may be that you, as the Caretaker, become exhausted and hopeless. Or the BP/NP may act out in even more dramatic and upsetting ways that push you toward the awareness that something is seriously wrong, and you begin to see that your bargaining solutions just aren't working. Then you may find yourself dropping into the stage of depression.

DEPRESSION

When everything you try results in the problems still going on and on with-out resolution, you start feeling hopeless and lose your belief that things will change. Disappointments mount up, logical "solutions" fail over and over, none of the changes you tried have really worked for long, the BP/NP doesn't change, and you become overloaded and less and less able to cope. More and more, you are seeing that you are not able to *make* the relationship change. You become aware that the BP/NP really is unmovable. You may lose faith in your own sense of reality and become hopeless about finding a solution to the misery that by now everyone in the family is feeling. You may also find yourself feeling significantly depressed or anxious or having physical symp-toms, such as panic attacks, migraines, overeating, and even heart stress. You are faced with having to give up your dreams of what you thought this relationship could be and of who you thought the BP/NP could be if he or she were healthy. Even your image of who you thought you were is deteriorating, and you come to realize how little you are able to do to make things better.

Getting to the stage of depression is actually a sign that you are coming to the real awareness that nothing you have been doing is going to change the BP/NP or this relationship. It is sad to lose all of these dreams, and the hopelessness of this awareness is depressing. But it is also a sign that you are seeing the relationship dynamics more clearly and realistically. Anyone liv-ing in the circumstances of caretaking a mentally ill person for so long and with so little self-care and support would obviously be depressed. Anyone trying to deal alone with the unreality and distortions of the BP/NP's world would ultimately become depressed. Anyone trying to function with only the skills that work in normally healthy families will inevitably fail when trying the same things with a BP/NP.

The stage of depression is actually a sign that you are coming to terms with your inability to cure or change the BP/NP and that you are ready to give up the cycle of denial, anger, and bargaining. You become willing to look at your situation in a new way. Perhaps you will be ready to try more radical changes in yourself and the way in which you participate in the relationship dance with the BP/NP. The part that *you* play in the relationship is the only thing that *can* be changed, and it is at this point, in the stage of depression, that you become more willing to take entirely new actions. How-ever, the actions you need to take to change the relationship are so counterin-tuitive that it can be very difficult to see what changes need to be made.

ACCEPTANCE

You start moving into the stage of acceptance when you realize that you are powerless to change the BP/NP. Acceptance can actually bring a sense of relief and calmness. It is at this stage that you finally understand that there is nothing that you can do to fix the behaviors, feelings, or thinking of the BP/NP. This understanding brings a sense of calm because now you know there is no longer any need to be angry at yourself or the BP/NP. There is no longer any need to put energy, thought, and time into giving in, placating, demanding, or tricking the BP/NP to make things work better. And there is no longer any need to continually work on understanding why the BP/NP does what he or she does.

Part of the goal of this book is to help you get to this place of acceptance. The relationship with the BP/NP can never be normal. It will always be a relationship in which you are dealing with a mentally ill person. The questions then become these: Do you *want* to continue to take care of this person? How can you take care of someone without continuing to be the Caretaker you have been? Are there more effective ways to deal with the BP/NP than what you have been doing? What changes in yourself could you make to have a better life either with the BP/NP or without him or her. How can you watch the BP/NP behave as he or she does and no longer have it send you through the stratosphere? How can you create a healthy life for yourself despite the BP/NP's illness? How can you deal sanely with the rage, anger, passive-aggressive behaviors, and manipulation of the BP/NP?

These and many other questions will be the focus of the rest of this book. Getting to acceptance may be a long struggle, but it is the gateway to getting your life in order and creating a new way of living that is more enjoyable, more productive, and more humane for yourself, your children, and the BP/NP. You also have to deal with the acceptance of *your* part in maintaining some of the negative aspects of the relationship with the BP/NP. This is not the same as the self-blame that you may already have been doing too much of.

Acceptance ultimately means that you finally realize that any change that occurs in the relationship with the BP/NP will have to be done by you. This can be overwhelming. However, it is also the key to understanding that you *do* have power in the relationship and that you *can* make changes, just not in the ways that you previously thought. Acceptance that borderline personality disorder and narcissistic personality disorder are lifelong mental illnesses can also provide the insight that can help you let go of your anger, hurt, and sense of powerlessness. Knowing what to realistically expect from the BP/NP and how to handle the situation puts you in a brand-new position compared to when you were trying to fix things from the Caretaker role.

You may still not like the behaviors of the BP/NP, but when you have reached acceptance, you finally see the situation in a different light. If borderline and narcissistic personality disorders can't be "cured," then you aren't responsible for curing them. Knowing and accepting that you have done the best you could, under extremely difficult circumstances, can help you stop blaming yourself. This can help you develop better self-esteem and a greater sense of direction with power over your life so that you can start feeling better about yourself and realize that you can become the director of your own life.

This is where Kubler-Ross's stages end. I have identified three more stages that I believe are part of the Caretaker healing process. In order to change from caretaking to self-care, you need to set boundaries, let go, and rebuild.

SETTING BOUNDARIES

Learning and being ready to set boundaries requires a change in your beliefs and attitudes as well as a set of skills that you will have to use regularly in order to move out of the Caretaker role. You cannot move toward the goal of good self-care without setting some new and solid boundaries. In fact, you cannot even have a clear sense of yourself and your own life without boundaries.

Boundaries are the invisible separations between yourself and others. They identify where you (your thoughts, feelings, responsibilities, wants, and needs) begin and end. In the relationship with the BP/NP, there has been a crazy-making rule that there should be no boundaries between you and the BP/NP. Setting boundaries is an important way for you to acknowledge and validate that you are a unique person with your own needs, rights, and life perspective. Having boundaries as a separate person is essential to your being able to know when you are being loved, valued, and respected for who you are and to tell when that is not happening..

By identifying that "I am this, not that" or that "I believe this, not that," you are identifying who you are. There is no one else in the world who is you. If you have only one life to live, then doesn't it make sense to be completely who you are?

You and the BP/NP are not *one*. You are not even very much alike. Caretakers make themselves blend in with the BP/NP. You are good at matching another person. You have been willing to accommodate the needs of the BP/NP at the expense of your own needs. You have lived your relationship with the BP/NP being enmeshed and without boundaries in order to keep the BP/NP calm and cooperative. Now, instead of spending all your time and energy focusing on and monitoring the BP/NP, you need to start setting boundaries by focusing on "I want," "I feel," "I need," "I like," "I don't like," and so on. These are the first boundaries you need to establish on your journey to manifesting yourself in the world.

When you begin setting boundaries, you begin defining and protecting your sense of self, rather like the skin does for the body. And like skin, having boundaries protects your sense of self from foreign elements that could cause you harm, such as other people's feelings, opinions, demands, and priorities. With boundaries, it will be easier for you to identify and follow your own inner needs, identity, and life. Setting boundaries is a real and significant change to the relationship with the BP/NP. Techniques for setting boundaries are outlined in later chapters.

General ways of setting boundaries include saying "No," making decisions and choices of your own, staying with your own feelings even when someone you care about has different feelings, solving only your own problems, and using your beliefs and opinions to structure and direct your life. This is a whole new way of being. Setting boundaries is a significant step toward moving from caretaking into self-care.

LETTING GO

You finally begin letting go as you start setting boundaries that are clear, defined, and consistent. In the letting-go stage, you stop your intense focus and overinvolvement with the BP/NP. In the past, you focused your entire attention, choices, and behaviors around the needs of the BP/NP. When you take responsibility for your own self-care, you begin letting go of responsibility for the BP/NP.

What does letting go mean in everyday terms? In means that you will *not* be changing who you are, what you think, what you like, or what you feel because of the desires and wishes of the BP/NP. Letting go requires that you relinquish your old need to please, appease, and control the BP/NP. Letting go requires that you have boundaries that are strong enough so that you can allow the BP/NP to be, act, or feel however he or she wants without you trying to change him or her. And you no longer allow the BP/NP to change these things in you. If you choose to have a relationship with the BP/NP, it will be based on the two of you being different, not being alike. Later chapters of this book will explain how you might accomplish this.

Letting go is very important to releasing your feelings of anxiety and depression. If it is no longer your responsibility who and what the BP/NP is and you no longer need to match the BP/NP in any way, then the pressure to be perfect, to please the BP/NP, or to fix or improve the BP/NP, is no longer necessary. This takes a huge load off of your shoulders and allows you to have the energy and enthusiasm to focus on good self-care.

REBUILDING

The last stage of healing from caretaking to self-care is a process of rebuilding your individuality, your sense of self-esteem, and your belief in your right to be *you*. Rebuilding empowers and stabilizes your sense of self by creating a life of your own design. It may include making friends with healthy people, changing your self-talk from negative to positive, loving yourself and treating yourself lovingly, letting go of anxiety and moving out of depression, increasing your interpersonal skills, and looking at yourself and your world in a new, freer way in order to create a life you love. This is all possible when you are taking care of yourself instead of caretaking the BP/NP.

Your sense of self is the psychological structure inside of you built from your genetic gifts, life skills, dreams, physical and emotional experiences, thoughts, needs, and yearnings for your own life. No one else on this earth has the same self as you do. Your life should be a legacy of who you are. And it is your primary responsibility to protect, nurture, and express your individual self. Your former caretaking behavior required you to give up this sense of self and to not develop or protect it. Don't worry—you can still be caring *of* others as you care for yourself, but do not care for others and abandon yourself, as that results only in your not honoring the gift of your unique life.

Just as the first four stages of denial, anger, bargaining, and depression cycled over and over until acceptance was reached, so do the last three stages of setting boundaries, letting go, and rebuilding cycle over and over until true self-care is reached. See the diagram in figure 10.1 to help clarify the process.

SELF-CARE

Keep in mind that self-care does not keep you from being caring and respectful of others. In fact, people who truly love and care for themselves are the very best at being loving to others. The "Golden Rule" that many Caretakers live by says, "Do unto others what you would have them do unto you." You may have thought that what you were doing as a Caretaker was loving and giving, but ultimately it has really been a form of trying to control a situation that feels out of control. You were giving in order to be given to. You have had an agenda about what you wanted the BP/NP to give to you,

CARETAKER

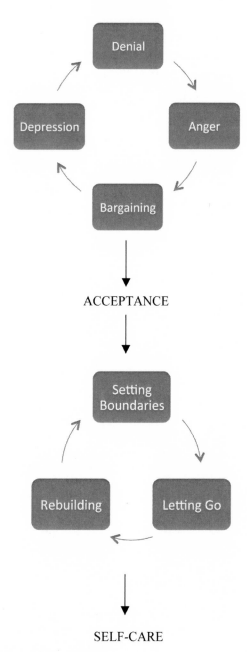

ACCEPTANCE

SELF-CARE

Figure 10.1.   Stages of Acceptance

and you gave it first, hoping that it would be reciprocated. You gave from a sense of your own neediness because you have not been caring for yourself.

Self-care sets up a reverse scenario. That is, you fill yourself up until you don't need the other person to fill you up. Then, whatever you give will come from a place of abundance rather than neediness. This keeps you from feeling that the other person *owes* you for what you give. It also makes you able to graciously receive as well as give. It honors and respects your own needs and individuality as it honors the BP/NP for who he or she is. In self-care, relationships are based on choice, love, respect, and acceptance of yourself and others just the way you are. The following chapters will explain this model further.

Chapter Eleven

Challenging the BP/NP Family Rules

ACCEPTING THE TRUTH

In order to stop being a Caretaker, you will have to confront and challenge the family rules that keep you at the mercy of the whims and needs of the BP/NP. Are you ready to stop living someone else's life with someone else's thoughts and feelings? Would you like to break the cycle of caretaking for your children's sake? Would you like to feel good about yourself, make your own decisions, and enjoy friendships and activities of your choosing? Would you like a peaceful, calm, relaxed life? Are you willing to take some brave steps to make that happen?

The only way to stop being a Caretaker is to stop playing the rescuer/persecutor/victim game with the BP/NP. If you want to have a sane life, you will have to break rules the BP/NP has set that keep you totally focused on him or her. It will take courage and determination to make these changes. But ask yourself, no matter how hard you tried to follow these insane rules perfectly, have you ever succeeded? Did all of your trying to please and rescue the BP/NP ever make any significant changes in him or her? Did it make the BP/NP a happier person? Did he or she love you more? Did you get along better? Does it even make sense that the relationship rules made by a mentally ill person would ever work? Of course not.

But which rules make sense, which rules work, and which don't? Start by writing down all of the rules about your relationship with the BP/NP. Look at the actual behaviors of the BP/NP and yourself and ask yourself the following questions:

Who has which responsibilities?
Who is allowed which feelings?
What must you agree about?

What is it okay to disagree about?

If there is a disagreement, how is a decision made?

Who makes the final decision for which things?

Who makes decisions about social activities?

If you disagree about a social activity, how is a decision made?

What emotions are you each allowed to express?

How are the finances handled?

As you can see, this isn't just about who does certain chores; it is more about how decisions are made and how you live your lives together. Keep focused on how your relationship actually works day to day, not how you pretend it is or hope it could be.

For example, one of the rules in my house growing up was that *you can't ask for anything you want.* I knew this was a rule because whenever *anyone* in the family asked for something, everyone else was allowed to tell him or her why he or she couldn't have it or shouldn't want it. It took me years to discover another, secret rule. I found out the secret rule when I finally had the courage to ask for something that I really wanted and kept asking past all of the reproofs from family members that I really didn't, shouldn't, or couldn't want it. The secret rule was this: *If you keep asking, they have to give it to you.* What a shock it was to discover this. It gave me a lot of courage to keep looking at the other rules about interactions in my family to discover how they really worked.

Once you have identified and written down the rules, the obvious ones and the secret ones, try to keep them clear in your mind and see if you can recognize them in new situations. Begin a plan to change, update, or elimi-nate the ones that don't actually bring health and goodwill to the relationship. This chapter will outline many common BP/NP rules and how to challenge them.

You already know that when you start breaking the BP/NP's rules, every-one will become very uncomfortable, and you may find the BP/NP upset at you. Keep in mind that you are making these changes to help everyone, including your children, yourself, and even the BP/NP. It helps if you always remain polite, firm, and determined. You know it will be very hard to tolerate not being liked or approved of, and the BP/NP knows this and will use it against you. Keep moving forward until you start seeing the changes you want. The following sections discuss challenges to the crazy-making rules that you will need to make to stop being a Caretaker.

YOU AND THE BP/NP ARE NOT ONE

You are not the same as the BP/NP. You do not have to be his or her clone. You have every right in the world to be who you are, to want what you want, and to have your own feelings. Breaking this rule of enmeshment, this rule of symbiosis, this demand of being a duplicate of the BP/NP, is *essential* in order to take the new actions discussed in this book and make your life better.

You may not have been aware that thinking, acting, and feeling alike is the most important and most powerful rule of the BP/NP because it is so completely assumed by the BP/NP that this is how relationships must work, ought to work, and absolutely will work. Even the BP/NP can't see this rule; he or she just feels that it is the only way to survive. But this rule completely annihilates any chance of you being a whole, healthy, happy human being because it annihilates your identity. This is what makes you so angry. It is what makes you so depressed. You, as a unique and individual human being, do not exist as long as you obey this rule.

You and the BP/NP are separate and different, and you will continually have differences of view, differences of opinions, different feelings, different wants, and different needs. You will have to overcome your fears of the BP/NP's anxiety, anger, and abject hostility as you make your choice to be a person in your own right.

Now is the time to decide if you can and will break the rule of sameness with the BP/NP. The rule resides within you as much as within the BP/NP. No two people can be exactly the same, not even if you were identical twins, which you are a long way from being. Your view of the world is very different. Your wants and needs do not need to be stunted by the mental illness of the BP/NP. Your depression and anxiety are symptoms of your internal sense of self wanting to be free, wanting to be expressed, and wanting to just be you. You cannot move forward with the ideas in this book until you come to terms with challenging this insane rule.

ACCEPTING THE FACTS

The BP/NP is mentally ill and will not get better in the foreseeable future. This is a fact that is denied by the BP/NP (he or she thinks that you are the crazy person), and you have colluded in this distortion. You have to give up your hope and fantasy that, with your help and direction and giving in and putting up with all that goes on, the BP/NP will somehow get better. As long as you stay in the Caretaker role, you are reinforcing the insane, dysfunctional behavior of the BP/NP. These are facts that you must come to see and accept.

You cannot change the BP/NP. You must accept the fact of your limitations, and you must accept the BP/NP just the way he or she is. How? What other choice do you really have? Until now, you may have been adamantly determined not to accept the mental illness of the BP/NP because his or her behavior is so infuriating and irritating and must be on purpose. But has all the trying, demanding, pleading, or giving in that you have done ever led to any kind of change in the BP/NP? Did your wanting the BP/NP to change make any difference? Did your anger at the BP/NP change anything? You probably wouldn't be reading this book if your need, want, or desire for the BP/NP to change had ever made any difference. It is time to accept that the BP/NP is not able or willing to change. At the same time, you need to accept that how you feel, who you are, and what you want are just the facts of your life as well and are equally valid.

It is only after you give up denial, anger, and bargaining; give up any hope of the BP/NP's being different; give up expecting the BP/NP to do what you want; and accept the real facts of the situation that you can finally start generating ideas that could make your life better. It is only after you quit focusing on what "should" or "shouldn't" be happening that you can really get down to what "is" or "isn't" happening. Basing your life on what you *hope* will happen rather than what *is* happening has been part of the reason for how you ended up being so frustrated, angry, and hurt. This is not to discount that some of the experiences you have had with the BP/NP were quite unpleasant and disturbing. But a lot of the angst, confusion, and indecision has been the result of the conflict in your own mind between what you think *should* be happening and what *is* happening and between what you and the BP/NP *pretend* is happening and what *is* happening.

YOU DON'T NEED THE BP/NP'S APPROVAL

The biggest power the BP/NP has over you comes from your fear of his or her, drama, blaming you for his or her feelings, criticisms of you, and threats of leaving. If the BP/NP holds over you threats of violence to him- or herself, you, or the children, that is a signal for you to get the BP/NP to a mental inpatient facility as soon as possible. Call 911, call the BP/NP's therapist and physician, and get yourself and the children to safety. *Do not* get into denial with yourself that the BP/NP is not serious and will not take action. *Do not* think that you can handle this situation yourself! One of the biggest mistakes Caretakers make is not taking threats of *violence* from the BP/NP seriously enough. Remember that you are dealing with a serious mental illness, even though much of the time the BP/NP looks and acts pretty normal.

On the other hand, Caretakers often take the BP/NP's acting out in rage, screaming, crying fits, and threats of leaving *too seriously*. Too often, Caretakers are many times more afraid of the BP/NP's rage than of his or her threats of violence. As a Caretaker, you have become hypervigilant to the emotional reactions of the BP/NP. However, you are reinforcing the BP/NP's behavior when you collapse in the face of his or her anger. If you give in to the BP/NP's demands, he or she will demand more. If you take the blame for the BP/NP's actions, he or she will blame you even more.

You have to learn to stand calm and steadfast. Do not be defensive. Do not take the putdowns and emotional attacks of the BP/NP as meaning anything about you. Do not seek forgiveness for "causing" the BP/NP's upset. Do not fall into amnesia about the volcanic behaviors you've witnessed in the BP/NP. Do not feed the BP/NP's emotion cycle. The fact that you don't have these same interactions with friends or colleagues at work is the indicator that you don't cause them to happen. Therefore, get centered and get clear in your mind so that you can see how your own fears get you to feed into the BP/NP's manipulations. It is your own pain and fear of the BP/NP's disapproval that lures you into their disastrous emotional hurricane.

What the BP/NP says, thinks, and feels about you or what he or she accuses you of during the throes of an emotional storm may or may not be true. But they are always irrelevant to the facts at the moment. At the moment of rage and anger, the BP/NP is in a delusion, is not rational, is "out of his or her mind." So take nothing the BP/NP says or does during these times as relevant about you, him or her, or reality.

Seek approval for your sense of self from the facts of your own actions and decisions, not from the ranting of a person inside an emotional nightmare. Seek your validation from friends, coworkers, your therapist, and other rational people who can give you feedback on who you are and whether you are acting with kindness or selfishness. Being in a therapy group for family members of BP/NPs can be amazingly helpful for getting validation, strength, and support in handling this crazy-making relationship you are in. Create and get support for your self-esteem outside your relationship with the BP/NP; do not expect the BP/NP to be able to give you support when you need it and do not expect to get an accurate reading of your value from the BP/NP.

CHANGE HOW YOU COMMUNICATE

BP/NP communication is often vague, convoluted, and confusing, starting out with one topic and morphing into a dozen or more topics with no conclusions and no decisions made at the end. You may find yourself agreeing to things you don't agree with or thinking that one conclusion has been made but the BP/NP insists it was a different conclusion. This type of communication is used to manipulate and control you into doing what the BP/NP wants.

If you want to talk clearly about something that is bothering you, a good process to follow is the Yale communication model. Use it first with yourself to clarify what you actually feel and want. Then try it with your children. It works extremely well with kids. Then move on to using it with friends and at work. When you feel competent in its use, try it with the BP/NP:

1. When _____ happens
2. I feel _____
3. I would like _____
4. Or I will need to _____

This model is a powerful means to communicate clearly with anyone and especially with highly sensitive or manipulative people. It conveys what you see is a problem, how you feel about it, and what you want. It is designed to be clear, concise, nonemotional, and nonjudgmental. Therefore, it is less likely to get off track and become attacking. It also does not require the BP/NP to do much of anything except listen. It is not a cure-all for every challenging communication with a BP/NP, but it is an effective tool.

The model begins with a *statement of an observable fact*, such as "When I see dirty clothes all over the living room . . . ," "When I hear a loud voice and sharp words . . . ," "When I get a statement in the mail saying the checking account is overdrawn . . . ," or "When I expect to have dinner at 5 p.m. and it isn't made until 9 p.m. . . ." Although you are saying statement to a particular person, notice that no one is specifically being blamed. This can waylay a defensive response from the other person while he or she waits to hear what you are going to say next. You will notice that the word "you" is purposely not used. Saying, "You are . . . ," "You did . . . ," "You always . . . ," "You never . . ." and so on is just an invitation to a fight. Leaving out "you" also lessens the desire of the other person to be defensive. Leaving out the word "you" can give you a chance to be heard, with less chance of the BP/NP being instantly defensive.

The next step is to *clearly state your own feelings about the event*. Saying, "I feel taken advantage of . . . " or "I feel angry, hurt, and humiliated" gives the other person information about how the event affected you. Again, you are *not* saying the word "you," nor are you saying that the other person "made you feel" this way. By taking responsibility for your own feelings, you are ending the blame game. You feel the way you do just because you do. Accepting your own feelings is an important step in getting others to take your feelings seriously. Being able to put your own feelings into words, to learn to know how things affect you, and to ultimately figure out what you want is also a significant way to validate yourself and feel more powerful.

With most people, you may not need much more than these two statements to make it clear what you feel. There is really nothing much more intimate than telling people how you feel. It is uniquely personal window into who you are. People who love you, respect you, and care about how you feel will respond with appropriate concern. They may actually ask you about the next step: *What do you want?*

The third step is letting the other person know what you want. "I would like to be talked to in a quiet voice," "I want this picked up right away," and "I would really appreciate your telling me ahead of time that you will be late" are all possible ways (from mild to strong) to convey your request for an action or a change in what is happening. When challenging a rule or the behavior of another person, it is more effective to be specific. Saying that you want to be "happy or supported or cared for" is too vague for the other person to actually know what to do differently.

Asking for what you want can be a challenge. You may find it hard to give yourself permission to ask for your wants to be considered. You may also think that by calling something a *need*, it will make it more important and powerful. However, the BP/NP is more affected by what you *want*. When you call something a need when it really is not, the BP/NP will challenge you and work to convince you that you don't actually need it. When you identify something as a *want*, it then becomes harder for the BP/NP to sound sane and reasonable if he or she tries to convince you that you don't actually want what you just said you wanted. Remember that the only other alternative to saying what you want is to manipulate and/or expect the other person to read your mind, or to give up the want altogether. To be an adult living the life you want to live, you have to have the courage to make polite requests of others to get what you want.

Before you move to the last step in the communication model, stop to see what the other person chooses to do. If the person is willing to cooperate at this point and do what you ask, great. Or this may be the time when the other person offers to negotiate, such as in the following examples:

"I'll talk more quietly, but I really want to deal with this issue now."
"I'm sorry I was late. I tried your cell phone, but it seems to be off."

Be on the lookout for passive-aggressive responses from the BP/NP, such as the following:

"You shouldn't feel that way."
"I don't see why you have to be so bossy."
"Everything is always about what you want."

Or there may be no response at all. These responses indicate a person who does not want to change, do any thing differently, or respect your feelings and wants. A healthy way to disagree with what you have requested is for the other person to say the following:

"I really don't want to do that."
"I'm not willing to take that action right now."

Straightforward disagreement allows the two of you to negotiate and perhaps find a third possibility that will be satisfactory to both of you. BP/NPs rarely negotiate because they feel certain that their own needs and wants will be ignored. They have learned to demand and grab to get their wants met. By using this new communication model, you may be able to introduce the idea of negotiation and demonstrate that you will listen to them as well as expecting to be listened to.

If the other person ignores you, says absolutely "no," or is passive-aggressive, you will need to consider using the last step in the model. The statement "Or I will need to . . ." is not to be used as a threat or a punishment. It is to be a statement of what you will do to *take care of yourself* without the cooperation of the other person, for example, "If you can't lower your voice, I will need to excuse myself from this conversation." *The most powerful tool you have at this point is to stop interacting with the other person.* You cannot be taken advantage of or forced to keep talking if you don't cooperate. The action you choose to take at this point must, obviously, be under your control and not depend on the other person doing anything more. This is the key to creating change in any relationship. You always have control over changing how available you are and what you decide to think and do. Keep in mind that you *must follow through* with what you say you will do, or you will not be taken seriously in the future. Here are some examples:

1. "When the subject is changed so many times, I get confused.
2. I feel lost, and I would really like to be able to discuss our different options.
3. I would like to focus on one topic to discuss right now. [wait for response]
4. Otherwise, I will have to continue this discussion another time when I am not so confused."

Here's another example:

1. "I'm not feeling that I'm having much fun here at the party.
2. I've decided I'd like to go home.
3. What would you like to do? [wait for a response]
4. So I'm going to head on home now."

Here's another:

1. "When I come home at 10 p.m. from class and see that the kitchen still needs to be cleaned up from dinner,
2. I feel disappointed.

3. I would really like it to be cleaned up by morning so that I can make breakfast. [wait for a response]
4. Or I won't be able to make pancakes in the morning."

This model works best when you talk in a calm, confident, and relaxed voice without threats or any kind of hysteria. You also must be willing to face unexpected challenges. No one can absolutely predict the behavior of another person, so be prepared to focus on taking care of yourself no matter what the other person decides to do. Be prepared to hear "no," be prepared for the BP/NP to be upset or unhappy in some way, be prepared to let the other person speak up for what he or she wants without rescuing or automatically giving in, and be prepared for the BP/NP to make irrelevant comments to get you off topic.

Follow through by taking care of yourself the way you said you would. If you say you will take a new action and then you don't follow through, this gives the BP/NP the message that your needs and wants aren't serious. If you are serious about making your life better, think through what you are willing to do, make a plan, and take these new actions.

YOU HAVE THE RIGHT TO SAY "NO"

It is extremely difficult to say "no" to a BP/NP. The word "no" sets you apart from the BP/NP. You are drawing a line in the sand that identifies your wants and needs as separate from those of the BP/NP. It conveys the message, "I don't agree; I have a different thought or feeling; I am not the same as you." There can be some strong reactions from the BP/NP to your standing up for yourself, including the following:

You may be threatened, called names, yelled at, or demanded that you agree.
You may be ignored as the BP/NP pretends you didn't say "no."
You may be mystified by being told that you don't really mean what you said.
You may be coerced by threats of abandonment or name-calling to change your mind.

Therefore, when you decide to say "no," you must be prepared to face your own inner guilt demons that will be triggered by the comments from the BP/NP. Here's a very simple, everyday example of what saying no might look like. The BP/NP starts out with the following:

"Would you like another piece of pie?"
"No thank you." [you're being very polite]
"Of course you would. I loved it."

"No thank you." [you keep repeating without explanation]

"Why don't you want another piece?"

"No thank you." [just keep going]

"Here. Another small piece won't hurt you." [putting it on your plate]
You've never liked anything I make."

"No thank you." [smile and don't eat it]

"Why aren't you eating your pie? You really hate me, don't you?"

"No thanks." [you don't get engaged in a dialogue]

You can see that this could go on quite a while, maybe even with other family members joining in the questioning and demanding to get you back into the Caretaker role. This would be a really good time to change the subject, get up and go to the bathroom, or ask someone else a personal question about themselves. These diverting tactics actually work pretty well with the BP/NP. If the level of emotion goes down, the BP/NP can often be sidetracked.

The real challenge in this exercise is to battle your *own* sense of guilt because you may be thinking that you are being obstinate, hurting the BP/NP's feelings, being ungrateful, not remembering the starving children in Africa, and so on. You may have been trained to feel that it is practically immoral to say "no" when someone in your family makes a request of you, no matter how trivial. Keep practicing. Move from saying "no" to food, to "no" to an activity you don't want to do, and to "no" to a life you no longer want. Sometimes the pressure to give in can be very powerful and painful, especially when the BP/NP is joined by another, powerful BP/NP in your life, such as the following example:

> Francine came into our counseling session saying that she was getting a lot of pressure from her mother to get back with her estranged husband. "I told her, 'Mom, do you really want me to get back with Danny? He's alcoholic, he let our seven-year-old son see pornography, he yells at me and hit me. I don't want to get back together with him.' You know what she said? She said, 'I'm sure he's learned his lesson. And he was so nice to me the other night when I saw him at the grocery store.' Well, he's not nice to me, I told her. Then she added, my own mother, 'Well, you are just being too picky.' Can you believe that?"

Even though another family member or a friend may pressure you to give in, it is very important that when you pick a battle, you stick with it. Otherwise, you give the message to the BP/NP that you really don't mean what you say.

Although the pressure from the BP/NP can be strong, it is really your internal sense of being undeserving, believing that you are selfish, or your own discomfort at displeasing others that really gets you to back down. Look closely at the ways you talk yourself out of saying "no." Why do you deserve less than others? What about saying "no, thank you" is selfish? Why can't you risk the BP/NP being displeased? The answers to these questions are important. Work on them.

YOU HAVE THE RIGHT TO ASK FOR WHAT YOU WANT

Asking for what you want is very similar to saying "no." It, again, places you outside the enmeshment with the BP/NP. You may have learned that just asking for what you want is being too selfish or hurting others. As a Caretaker, it may seem very strange to ask others for the very things you so easily give. You may actually feel like you are imposing on others. Or you may think that someone who loves you should just give these things to you without your having to ask, but that is just because you feel bad for asking. Why do you deserve less? Why is it imposing to ask a loved one for a caring behavior? Why does asking scare you?

To challenge the "nonasking" rule of the BP/NP, you may need to start small and increase the importance of your requests as you get stronger. First, practice with a trusted friend or gentle family member before attempting to challenge the BP/NP. Here's the experience of Jenn (married 18 years):

"I can't tell you how many beers over the years my husband has asked me to get him when I was sitting right there next to him watching the same TV program. So I decided I'd ask him for a glass of water when he went into the kitchen the next time. I was amazed at how hard it was for me to ask and not just jump up myself and get it. But I did ask. And he just said, 'Sure, OK' and brought it to me. It was so surprising that such a little thing like that made me really like him a whole lot more. I just assumed he wouldn't agree to do it. But it didn't faze me a bit. I felt like I was actually important to him."

DON'T GIVE REASONS OR EXPLAIN YOUR DECISIONS

When you decide to do something different from the BP/NP, whether it is being alone sometimes, dressing differently, reading different books, liking different foods, and so on, you will be making yourself vulnerable to a lot of coercion to change your mind. Being different is seen by the BP/NP as being "wrong" and can trigger your fears that the BP/NP will reject or try to humiliate you for leaving the enmeshed "us-ness." But if you have worked on approving of yourself instead of getting approval from the BP/NP, you will be able to move forward.

One of the most common ways the BP/NP tries to convince you to get back into the "right" way of doing things is to question your reasoning. "Well, why would you want to do that?" "Why do you feel that way?" The tactic of getting you to explain yourself is a means of getting information that the BP/NP can use to prove to you that your choice, your feeling, your want, and even you as a person are wrong.

Believe it or not, you do not have to give people reasons or explanations for what you do, unless *you* want to. This may be a startling revelation if you have spent years around a BP/NP. You really do not have to give detailed reasons and explanations to anyone for what you want to do. The BP/NP's need to be in control of all the information around them is often extreme, but you don't have to buy into it.

I was seeing a client, Nora, with severe borderline disorder, when I got pregnant. My husband and I had waited until the third month, so we were pretty certain the pregnancy would go to term before I told my clients. I decided I would tell Nora first since I felt it might take her more time to deal with this change in our therapeutic relationship. I had read in a couple of studies that said BP clients often feel that they are going to be abandoned by the therapist who gets pregnant.

I told Nora during our next session that I was pregnant and would be taking four months off after the birth and suggested that we start talking about her therapy needs during those months before I would be returning. She looked horrified and demanded that I tell her what day I had gotten pregnant and why I hadn't told her immediately. I ignored the content of her question and asked her what her concerns were. She then wanted to know why I hadn't told her I was intending to get pregnant during her therapy. Again, I asked what concerned her, and she then blurted out her fear that I was going to die in childbirth and never come back to be her therapist.

If I had given her reasons for getting pregnant or responded to her questions, it would have put the focus of the therapy onto me and made my personal issues vulnerable to her demands. Instead, I kept the focus on her fears, and we sidestepped the circular demand/explain dance that could have ensued and would have derailed our therapy relationship even more than my absence of a few months.

BP/NPs have a lot of fears and anxieties when anything and anyone around them changes, but you can respond to their "why" questions by asking about their fears and concerns or simply stating again and again, "This is something I like to do, and I hear that it is different from what you like to do."

Not giving a reason or explaining your decisions gives you control over your own thoughts, feelings, and actions. It allows you to state who you are without getting into a debate about right and wrong. You are refusing to participate in giving or receiving manipulation, invalidation, and rejection.

TAKING ACTION

Stop Talking

Very little gets changed with a BP/NP by talking. BP/NPs are masters of denial and delusion. They jump instantaneously from topic to topic, they are emotional rather than logical, and they usually forget any discussion that has been emotionally intense. Making changes in the relationship with a BP/NP requires taking new actions, not making agreements or coming to an understanding.

In order to take new actions, you will have to decide what you want to do differently. Look at what you want to be different in your own life and start figuring out what actions you need to take to head your life in that direction. Some examples are the following:

> If you want your BP/NP partner to quit making false promises, quit asking for promises.
>
> If you want to quit having fights with the BP/NP, don't respond defensively and don't argue; rather, use the communication model.
>
> If you want something done and the BP/NP stubbornly refuses to do it, do it yourself.
>
> If you want to be more social than the BP/NP, go out with friends by yourself.
>
> If you don't like living with the BP/NP, live apart.
>
> If the BP/NP criticizes or devalues you, do not accept it as a statement about you.
>
> If a conversation is going nowhere positive, quit conversing.

When you see clearly what is going on and you know clearly what you want, it is easier to figure out what to do even without the cooperation of the BP/NP.

BREAK OUT OF THE DRAMA TRIANGLE

The most important action that you need to take to quit caretaking is to break out of the Drama Triangle. This means that you are going to quit taking on the roles of victim, persecutor, and rescuer. All of these roles require one person to be superior, right, good, and better than the other person, while the other person has to be inferior, wrong, bad, and worse. This one-up/one-down game has to be stopped in order for you to stop caretaking. Caretaking is the epitome of your thinking and acting like you know better and are more capable than the BP/NP and therefore that you have the right to control, direct, and improve the BP/NP or, conversely, that you should be the one to always give in. At the same time, the BP/NP continually tries to control, direct, and improve *you* so that you will merge with and match his or her thoughts and feelings. The following steps can help you move out of the Drama Triangle thinking and acting.

Refuse to be Superior or Inferior

You have to be willing to stop playing the superior/inferior Game with the BP/NP in order to really make changes. Almost all interactions with the BP/NP are based on who is better than/worse than, right/wrong, deserving of blame/deserving of defense, who gets more/who gets less, and so on. Playing the persecutor, victim, or rescuer is always a game of superior/inferior.

Breaking the rule of superior/inferior requires you to learn to accept differences and similarities between yourself and others as neither good nor bad. This will allow you to come to terms with what you like and don't like. If you take responsibility for your own decisions and allow the BP/NP to do the same, then neither one of you has to be good or bad.

Breaking the superior/inferior game of the Drama Triangle is a very big step to take. What does it look like to live without succumbing to superior and inferior feelings about yourself and others? It means giving up being the rescuer, the victim, and the persecutor forever. It means being totally responsible for yourself and not for the BP/NP. You make your own decisions and have your own feelings and actions, thoughts, and interpretations. It means you will see yourself and the BP/NP as unique individuals with your own different strengths and abilities, weaknesses, and lack of skills without seeing either of you as better or worse than the other, completely without the judgment of right or wrong. It means you don't collapse into being a victim of the BP/NP; you don't try to fix, improve, or persecute the BP/NP or yourself; and you no longer try to help or rescue the BP/NP. It means you will accept yourself and the BP/NP just as you are. It is only then that you can come up with solutions and interactions that are effective for you and your family.

Stop the "Poor Me" Game: Stop Being a Victim

Ignoring your own wants and needs, denying your own opinions, giving in to whatever the BP/NP wants even if it is harmful, taking the blame for everything, and giving up who you are and how you want to live are all ways that Caretakers get stuck in the victim role. Although you may think you are being nice and being helpful, you are merely perpetuating the BP/NP's rules and the dysfunctions in your family. It is also a way for you to not feel responsible for your own timidity and fearfulness in the interactions between you and the BP/NP. It leads to a sense of passivity and powerlessness that ultimately keeps you from taking the actions that you could take to make your life different, that is, happier, healthier, and freer. When you start feeling overwhelmed, unable to cope, depressed, and wanting to isolate, you are moving into the victim role.

When you begin to refuse being the inferior, the victim, you begin the journey to breaking the Drama Triangle. There are many more possible roles and behaviors to take than the three that have been allowed up to now in your relationship. You have the capacity to step back and think of what you really feel, what you really want, and what actions could get you going in a new direction. The BP/NP can't or won't step out of these designated roles, but you could choose to do so and change the game entirely.

In order to stop being a victim, you will have to be willing to accept the actual circumstances of your relationship with the mentally ill BP/NP. You have to face the fact that if anything is going to change, you will have to be the one to make the changes. You will have to face your fears and take new actions. You will have to learn new skills and make new decisions. The following chapters are aimed at giving you the tools and understanding to make those changes.

Stop The Blame Game: Stop Persecuting

Living in a BP/NP relationship, you have learned to blame others. Breaking the rule of blaming others can be challenging because you may not really know how to ask someone to do something different. If you look back at the communication model, you will see the way to make this change.

Instead of telling the person, "You didn't wash your hands" or "You gave me the wrong papers," change the focus from what didn't happen to what you want. Even just using the "I want . . ." statement from the model is often enough, for example, "I'd like you to wash your hands before dinner" or "I'd appreciate it if you could find page 8 for me." Giving directions and telling others what you want rather than blaming them for doing things wrong shows them how to be successful and feels a lot better, too. You are also more likely to get more cooperation from others.

It also means you will take responsibility for how you act and feel around the BP/NP without taking the attitude that the BP/NP is controlling your feelings or actions. This means that if the BP/NP does something you don't like, you say or do something about it. You acknowledge that you are choosing how you respond, emotionally and behaviorally, without blaming the BP/NP for causing your feelings and actions.

Stop Fixing and Rescuing the BP/NP

Being a Caretaker may have been your lifelong role/identity, so it could be a hard habit to break. You have felt obligated to do it. You have felt guilty for not doing it. You may have needed to do it with a BP/NP parent to make your life as a child bearable. You may have enjoyed the superior status of being the helper, the good person, and so on. It may be very hard to relinquish the false hope that the BP/NP will someday step permanently into the role of a responsible and giving adult, partner, or parent. You have to face your own outdated fantasies, feelings, and beliefs and let them go before you can stop fixing, rescuing, and caretaking the BP/NP.

You have been the Caretaker as a way to keep the peace, keep the delusion, keep your fantasy, keep the family together, keep the BP/NP calm, and so on. But face it: none of your caretaking methods have worked for more than a few minutes or a few days anyway.

Giving up rescuing the BP/NP is an action, not a discussion. It isn't something to announce to the BP/NP. It isn't something to negotiate with the BP/NP. It isn't something to threaten the BP/NP with. It is all action. You stop participating in the merry-go-round interactions, you stop arguing, you stop worrying what the BP/NP will do next, and you stop expecting the BP/NP to fulfill your needs. This does not mean that you have to stop caring about or loving the BP/NP. You change from being a rescuer in the interaction by making choices and taking actions that work better for you and that might even work better for the BP/NP. It could look like this:

> Linda had been quite frequently affected by her BP mother's overemotionality, lack of ability to see Linda as a separate person, and general lack of nurturing and attention. When Linda started therapy, she was hurting and fearful and was a loyal and intensely perfect Caretaker of her mother. After about a year of therapy focused on Linda's letting go of the Caretaker role as well as her expectation of ever being emotionally seen and heard by her mother, Linda came into a session and told me about spending most of the day before taking her mother on a round of errands:
>
> "It was totally my choice to help my mother. She's going on a trip, and I know she is a whacked out, emotionally hysterical person. She was getting very anxious, and I asked her if she would like me to drive her around to get things done. In the past I would have done it so I could try to get her to see me as a good daughter or because I thought I should protect my dad from her getting angry and refusing to go on the trip with him. This time, I had a free afternoon, and I just wanted to help her feel more calm. I drove because her driving would have made us both crazy. Usually her telling me where to turn, what lane to be in, and where to park would upset me, but it didn't this time because I knew it was my choice. That is just how she is, and I knew that when I took this on. I did set a clear rule that if she screamed or began berating me when she got scared in the traffic, I would pull over until she could get herself calm, and I made it clear we would go home if she did it more than once.
>
> "She was delighted I was volunteering to help her. She only screamed once, and I pulled over. The day went pretty well after that, and she even thanked me and said she couldn't have gotten it all done without my help. I felt so good that I was in control and that I could handle a difficult interaction with my mom as a real adult, and it worked."

Linda now knows her mother will never be the mother she wanted. She is still dealing with leftover hurt and anger, but she has clearly taken on responsibility for how she interacts with her mother. She knows it is up to her to make whatever changes will happen in her life and in her relationship with her mother. This is the only mother she will ever have, and she is clear about what kinds of interactions she chooses. As a result, she can have a more positive relationship with her mother even though she has decided to make it much more limited in time together. She also feels much better about herself.

Start Using the Caring Triangle

It can be helpful to picture a new triangle to keep you focused on the new behaviors we have just discussed. Instead of the actions of the persecutor, you take on the new behaviors of doing and assertion. You give up trying to force others to do what you want and blaming them for what you don't like, and you take actions that you decide on. You ask for what you want, you act on your own behalf, and you take positive action.

Instead of the victim role, you accept the situation you are in and take responsibility and make choices to function in a more healthy and happy way. You put real thought into what you want and how to get it, and you take action to make things change.

Instead of being the rescuer, you give the BP/NP the respect of letting him or her take care of solving his or her own problems, dealing with his or her feelings, and choosing his or her own solutions. You can refuse to take what the BP/NP says and does as meaning anything about who you are. You can quit letting fear, obligation, and guilt control and manipulate you into taking care of the BP/NP when you really don't want to. Your attitude makes a huge difference in getting out of the Drama Triangle. The Caring Triangle is shown in figure 11.1.

KEEP AT IT, AND THINGS WILL START TO CHANGE

Setting out to challenge the BP/NP's rules and roles can seem daunting, but if you truly want to stop being a Caretaker and make your life better, it is up to you to make these changes. It may be smart to try out your new behaviors with non-BP/NP friends or family members first to observe the results. Practice until you feel you can stand firm in the midst of the BP/NP's hurt, anger, and fear. When the BP/NP can't get you to participate in the old rules and interactions, he or she can get pretty upset, at least for a while. If you think of the BP/NP's reaction more like that of a two-year-old having a temper tantrum, it may be easier for you to stick to your changes. And like most temper tantrums, they will pass, as Kevin found out.

CARING TRIANGLE

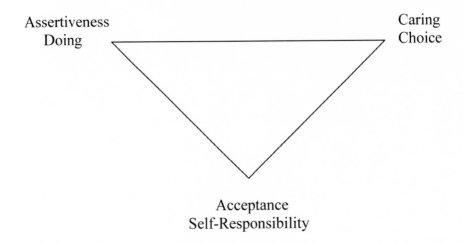

Figure 11.1.   **The Caring Triangle**

Kevin had been in therapy for several years before he decided that he was ready to let go of his overfunctioning, caretaking behaviors with his BP wife, Natalie. He finally decided that he was not going to let her fears about social situations keep him isolated. He realized that he had let his friendships dissolve from inattention, and he and Natalie had no couple friends at all. So Kevin told his wife that he was going to be spending Friday evenings after work with some of the guys from work, and he was going to attend social events at their children's school whether she went or not.

Natalie responded by accusing him of having an affair, of wanting to leave her, of being ashamed of her, of hating her, and so on. She also decided to fly home to Missouri to visit her sister. In the past, Kevin would have tried to defend himself, reassured her that he was faithful and that he loved her, and then he would have finally gotten angry and given up. He would have called her several times in Missouri to see how she was and to try to mend the breach. However, this time, Kevin was clear on what he wanted, and he had learned a lot about not doing the same old responses that had in the past resulted in no progress.

This time Kevin simply said, "I understand that you don't like social events very much, but I do like them. I like spending time with friends, and I have decided I am going to do that. I hope it will help you feel better to visit your family in Missouri." Natalie was gone for three weeks. Kevin did not call. He decided to follow through with his decision to be more social and went to several events during those three weeks. After a week, Natalie began calling every day. Kevin still did not initiate any calls, but he told her that he missed her and hoped she was having a good time. When Natalie arrived home, she made no mention of Kevin's meeting with friends and going to social events without her. She acted as if this had been the way it was all along. Kevin was astonished at how quickly this change was accepted and realized that he had never followed through with breaking the rules long enough to enact a change.

CREATE A LIFE FOR YOURSELF

The example above gives you a bit of an idea of what creating a life for yourself means. You are the only one who can decide how you want to live your life, and you are the only one who can make it happen. Quit expecting the BP/NP to like it, approve of it, or support it in any way. After you learn to withstand the BP/NP's disapproval and find that he or she usually gives in after a while, you will find that taking new actions (while not without anxiety) is doable. If the BP/NP has continually escalated, as you've taken some of the steps above, and ended up in the mental hospital or has threatened or abused you, creating your own life is most likely going to have to be done completely without the BP/NP.

Everything starts with you figuring out what you want to do with your life. How do you want to feel, think, and act? Start thinking about it now. Don't delay any more. Get busy thinking about yourself for once. Are you in the career you want? Are you living where you want? Do you have the friends you want? Are you enjoying your personal life? Are you being the parent you want to be?

Think about your children and what you have taught them about life through your past actions with the BP/NP. Is it what you want them to learn about relationships? Are they prepared to go out and create good lives for themselves? If your children copied what you have shown them with your life, would you be happy for them? Sometimes it is easier to start changes because you have a hope and vision for a better life for your children. But don't do it all for them. Let them be a catalyst of inspiration for your own changes.

You can change your life. It's not easy, but tens of thousands of Caretakers have left or improved their relationship with a BP/NP family member. You can too. Individual therapy and being in a Caretakers' recovery group will give you a lot of support and validation. If the BP/NP in your life is a coworker, a neighbor, a friend, or someone you are dating, you will probably find the suggestions in the book to be steps you can do fairly quickly and effectively.

If the BP/NP is your spouse or a parent, ask yourself whether this is a relationship in which you can find happiness with only the changes you can make or whether this a relationship that has already self-destructed. Make the changes and see what happens. When you are clear inside yourself about who you are and what life you choose to live, your relationship with a BP/NP will also become more clear. It may even get better.

Chapter Twelve

Beginning to Heal: Embracing New Beliefs and Behaviors

DON'T BELIEVE EVERYTHING YOU HEAR

If you have been a Caretaker for some time, you have probably read many self-help, personal advice, and improve-your-life books by now. You may have tried a lot of the suggestions in these books, and undoubtedly you've had some success in making your life better. I doubt, however, that you have been able to feel a whole lot better about your relationship with the BP/NP. And you may have begun to doubt your ability to function in healthy ways in intimate relationships.

Many of the ideas and suggestions in typical books on relationships as well as the advice of friends trying to be helpful are just not relevant to your situation. These ideas may not be for your situation because very few people really understand the dynamics of personality disorders. This chapter identifies what changes in your thinking and behaviors you need to consider when working with a BP/NP, and these can make a real difference in your unique family interactions.

WHAT IS NORMAL VERSUS WHAT IS HEALTHY

"Whatever normal is, I know my family isn't it," said Marie at our first session. "We look normal, we live in a normal house, and we pretend among ourselves that we're normal, but I know we aren't," she continued.

"How do you know that?" I responded.

"I've never felt normal," she responded.

It is not uncommon for Caretakers to wonder what is normal. You may feel there is *something* wrong with you. And you certainly know there is something wrong with your relationship with the BP/NP. Growing up with a BP/NP or being married to one is certainly not a normal experience.

The relationship with the BP/NP can frequently be chaotic, unpredictable, and overly emotional and rarely makes much sense. You may often be confused about whether something is wrong with you or with the BP/NP. If you already know there is something wrong with your BP/NP parent, adult child, or spouse, it can be very threatening to realize you are permanently attached to someone who is so dysfunctional. Therefore, it can actually feel more comfortable to think there is something wrong with you. At least then you can believe that you have control over changing it. So seeing yourself as *not normal* can be a way to stay safe and work at changing things without really making any waves with the BP/NP.

Your relationship with the BP/NP probably doesn't feel the way you think it should feel. It doesn't feel relaxed, or safe, or warm. You may have spent years trying to do something to make your relationship better with very little change happening. You know your relationship with the BP/NP is not normal, but you don't know what to do instead. Some of the signs that you are with a BP/NP are the following:

Family fights never change or improve the problem.
Adult conflicts look just like two kids fighting.
There is a lot of blaming of others.
There is no forgiveness.
Fights include sudden attacks and withdrawals.
Disagreements are dramatic, emotional, and threatening.

Since it is actually pretty hard to identify what is normal in intimate personal relationships because families vary greatly by culture, beliefs, religions, and areas of the country, it seems clearer to talk about what is healthy.

In relationships, healthy is what makes people feel good about themselves. So let's look at what makes people grow into healthy, functional, and productive human beings. What are behaviors, attitudes, and skills that truly work to create happiness and good feelings? What allows people to develop the willingness to be intimate? What creates the ability to look at reality and deal with it on a consistent basis? Think about what behaviors are needed to make your life more enjoyable on a long-term basis.

BP/NP-dominated families have lots of rules, rituals, and fixed behavior interactions to keep them stabilized. By working to become healthier and leave the Caretaker role, be aware that this could greatly disrupt your family and your relationship. You are stepping into a maturing process in yourself that eventually becomes irreversible. Whenever our understanding and our skills in the world increase and mature, we rarely, if ever, go back to being less aware or less skilled or wanting less of the good things that have come into our lives. After you learn to read or ride a bicycle or know that the earth is round or that water flows downhill, you cannot reverse and not know these things. Knowledge permanently changes how you view yourself and the world. Caterpillars turn into butterflies, not the other way around. You will be changing; however, it is very unlikely that the BP/NP will make very many changes.

THIS IS YOUR JOURNEY *ALONE*

Caretakers continually search for ways to change the BP/NP. You may have read self-help books, talked to friends, learned new communication skills, and even gone to therapy to figure out how to bring out the good person that you believe is inside the BP/NP. You may have had high hopes for the BP/NP. You may have nearly exhausted yourself trying to improve your relationship with the BP/NP, but searching for solutions to the BP/NP's *problem* does not work and cannot continue if you are to get healthy.

Right now, you have to decide to go on this healing journey for yourself and for yourself alone. Always trying to help someone else is just a way you keep from facing reality and making changes in your own life. You came into this life alone, and you will leave it at your own time. The life you are living is yours—alone. It is your job to make your life what you want it to be. It is not your job to make someone else's life what you want it to be.

Nothing you learn in this healing journey will directly help the BP/NP. One of the most important new rules you need to embrace is this understanding: *you cannot heal anyone else; you can heal only yourself.* You may find yourself already disagreeing or feeling angry about this assertion. It is not a rule that I made up. It is just how the universe works. For example, you may not like gravity, but gravity is a truth of this world whether you like it or want to believe it. It just is. Not being able to force or make someone else heal is just a fact. Think to yourself, Have I ever healed anyone? I've been a therapist for over 25 years, and I've never healed anyone. Many patients got better, but *they* did the work of healing, they kept themselves motivated, and they decided what and how to heal. I acted as their supporter and guide. If you are trying to change the BP/NP, you will not be fully focused on what you need to do, and you will fail, both with the BP/NP and with yourself.

FACING THE FACTS

Right now, you may not know what is realistic or true in your relationship. You have been in a delusional world for as long as you have interacted with the BP/NP. Part of your healing is facing the truth that the BP/NP is dysfunctional and may very well never get better. This can be a very depressing awareness.

However, it is only by looking at this fact and looking deeply inside yourself that you can identify what life you really want to create for yourself. You cannot expect or count on the BP/NP to make any changes. What do you want to do with that? Do you know your own strengths? Do you know how you hold yourself back from going toward the life you want? What are you willing to do to make your life what you want it to be? This requires you to stop looking at the BP/NP and focus on yourself.

YOU HAVE CONTROL ONLY OVER YOURSELF

Here is another uncomfortable truth: you have no control over anyone or anything else other than yourself. This may cause you to grumble or doubt. As a Caretaker, you have probably spent enormous amounts of time and energy trying to control the BP/NP's thoughts, feelings, and behaviors in order to make things better, but has it ever really worked? Sometimes it may have seemed to work, but I'll bet that was really the result of the random nature of the universe and that the changes didn't last.

If you could *really* control things outside of yourself, why can't you do it all the time? In fact, by focusing on trying to control things outside of yourself, you have probably not been fully and responsibly in charge of yourself. For instance, by putting too much energy into trying to get the BP/NP to change, you actually put yourself into a state of anger and resentment, or by trying to do everything perfectly, you lost sight of the fact that you didn't want to do what you were doing at all. So you cannot get what you want by focusing on making others change. Let's see what happens when you focus on changing only yourself.

YOU CAN CHANGE ONLY TWO THINGS

There are exactly two categories of things that you have the full power to change: your *behavior* and your *thoughts*. Most clients I work with really want to change the behaviors, beliefs, or feelings of someone else. However, these things are impossible to change because you do not have direct control over any of them.

If you can't control something, you can't directly change it. If you are not directly changing something, then you are manipulating or trying to coerce the change. For instance, when you have not felt loved by the BP/NP, have you tried to get him or her to love you by complaining, trying to please, demanding, begging, or threatening? Did it work? Did the BP/NP's love change toward you? How do you know for sure? Even if the BP/NP's behavior changed for a while, how much do you trust that it is changed for good?

The other thing most people want to change is how they *feel*. It can take quite a while and a lot of work to change how you feel because you can't *directly* alter your feelings. Again, you have to work by changing your behavior and thoughts, and then these changes affect how you feel. So if you want to feel happier, you have to take actions and direct your thoughts to things that create that happiness in you. See what I mean? From here on, I will be talking about *your* behavior and thoughts and what you can do to make your life the life you want to live.

YOU ARE NOT STUCK

Up to now, you may have felt stuck with a life you can't control and can't change. If you are trying to control the BP/NP, you are quite right—you are stuck. When you realize how much you can change by focusing on your own behavior and your own thoughts, the picture changes dramatically. You are not stuck.

In fact, as an adult, everything in your life is there because you choose it, you allow it, or you accept it. Now you may disagree and say, for example, that you didn't choose your mother, but I will tell you that you do allow and accept her behavior around you and that you could actually change what you allow and accept. The problem that makes you feel stuck is often that you don't like and don't want the responsibility of the consequences of your choices. BP/NPs can make the consequences of new thoughts and behaviors look really frightening. The BP/NP may yell, scream, manipulate, and threaten, but keep in mind that you are colluding with the BP/NP if you let your anxiety and fear alter your focus from your own life and your own options back on to him or her.

For years, I taught a university freshman family communications course and enjoyed talking to the students about this idea of choosing, allowing, and accepting. They were just moving from living under their parents' roof as children to being on their own in a dorm or an apartment and beginning to see themselves as adults. However, their behaviors and thoughts were still evolving, and they hadn't fully left the rules of childhood. They would often complain that their parents were still treating them like children, to which I would reply that they were probably not yet fully thinking or behaving like adults. This would set off lively discussions that would end in my challenging them to own their own power over their own thoughts and behaviors and to decide for themselves what they were choosing, allowing, and accepting from their parents.

A really common example was the complaint from students that their mothers called too often, and some of them did call daily or several times a day. Their initial attempt to solve the problem was usually to focus on changing Mom by telling her not to call so much, that is, to ask for the other person to change. Great idea. It is an adult behavior to politely ask other adults to change their annoying behavior toward you. When asked, about half of the moms did call less, but the other half didn't change.

The next step for most of the students was to try manipulation by getting angry, being rude, or pouting to get their point across. These tactics created no change whatsoever. So I would suggest that they look at what they could do to make a change in their own thoughts and behaviors. They weren't choosing to have Mom call so often, but they were allowing and accepting it. How could they, I asked, not allow or accept the calls? Typically, out of a class of 40 students, only one or two hands would go up to answer this question. Most of them could not fathom the thought that they had any power to not allow or not accept anything their parents did, nor did they have any idea about what they could do differently. To me the obvious suggestions were to 1) screen their calls and not answer, 2) wait to call back when the time was convenient for the student, and 3) limit the time the student talked to the parent by hanging up when they wanted to.

These constituted absolutely shocking thoughts and behaviors to some students, even though these were the obvious choices. Initially, these students would resist by saying that these behaviors wouldn't work, then they would go to "disaster vision" by saying that the parent would be too angry, might cut off their financial support, or would be disastrously emotionally damaged by the rejection.

A few students would move to abject terror or depression just thinking about this horrible disruption of their lives. Does this sound familiar? You guessed it. These were the Caretakers in the class. They felt stuck. Maybe you identify with some of this thinking and these fears in relation to the BP/NP in your life.

What was the result for the students who tried one of the options we discussed in class? *All* were successful in limiting the number of calls from Mom because the students were in control of answering, not answering or calling back. Ninety percent of them got *no* negative feedback from the parent at all, and the others who got complaints pretty easily dealt with those by explaining that they were busy studying.

The truth is that the BP/NP is not forcing you to allow or accept his or her behavior; it is really your own fears, worries, and beliefs that keep you trapped in the reciprocal interaction with the BP/NP. So, just like those freshmen, I ask you, Are you ready to take on adult behaviors so that you can decide to choose what your own life will be like?

ANY CHANGE IN YOU

Murray Bowen, the first family therapist, showed that it is a fact of relation-ships that everyone who participates in the relationship influences the actions of all the other participants to some degree. So, although you cannot directly change or control the behavior of the BP/NP, you can change your own thoughts and behaviors and get different reactions and results. Changing yourself, choosing more adult behaviors, acknowledging your own needs, asking others for what you want, and valuing yourself more all contribute to changing your life and everyone around you.

These changes may take the form of others treating you better, or it may be that some people no longer want to be around you or you no longer want to be around them. When you make changes, you are then in control of what you will and won't do, what you will and won't allow others to do to you, and what you will and won't accept from others.

Since you cannot directly change the BP/NP, it is important to remove your focus from what the BP/NP should change to what you can and want to change in order to create a better life for yourself. Changes in *you* are the cornerstone of changes in your relationships, living environment, self-es-teem, sense of freedom, and success in life.

FEELINGS ARE NOT FACTS

Just because you have certain feelings doesn't mean that those feelings are based on present reality or that you should act on them. Feelings are a combination of emotions (i.e., body sensations), memories, and thoughts. Feelings are highly changeable, and they are easily misinterpreted or mis-identified. For example, the feelings of excitement and fear may seem quite opposite of each other; however, they result from the same body sensation but with different interpretations. The freshmen above who felt too fearful to make new choices were interpreting their emotional sensations differently than the freshmen who left the class with some trepidation but that same week made new choices about talking with their parents and excitedly re-ported their success in the next class.

The BP/NP's feelings are not absolute facts either. They are frequently based on overly intense emotional sensations with disaster-oriented interpre-tations. In addition, many feelings are leftover reactions to experiences in the past that are no longer present. For example, if your BP dad flew into a rage every time you made a mistake, it does not mean that the feeling of fear that you have in the present of extreme danger when you make a mistake is realistic, appropriate for the setting, or helpful to your functioning or your safety. Don't automatically trust your feelings. Ask yourself if your feelings are based on present reality, on past experiences, or on fears you have about the future. Only then can you decide what actions you want to take to deal with the feeling.

An overly emotional reaction in yourself and in the BP/NP can lead to some poor choices and behaviors. Let yourself and the BP/NP calm down before making decisions. Feelings, even strong ones, don't last that long, but they do cloud good judgment. Start making choices on the basis of facts and goals rather than emotional reactions, and you will see marked improvement in your solutions.

THE PAST MAY NOT BE A HELPFUL PREDICTOR OF THE PRESENT

You need to learn to identify feelings that are based on present facts rather than memories, rules or delusions, and manipulated experiences from the past. Feelings based on manipulation, past responses from others, and past traumatic experiences are identifiable by their "over-the-top" expression. That is, they are too strong and too dramatic to be a response to a present feeling. When you hear yourself or other people say, "You're always doing that," "You are just like my mother," or "You never leave me alone," or when you or others have very dramatic responses (e.g., shouting, screaming, stomping around, hitting, and so on), these are feeling responses that are based on the past and not on the present.

Feelings from the past that come into the present are called *transference*. These are feelings that are being transferred from a similar experience with someone in the past to a present situation. As a result, the feelings are much bigger and more dramatic than they should be. They are triggered by an experience in the present, but they cannot be understood by looking at the present situation. Most people don't even know that their present-day over-reaction is really about unresolved feelings from the past.

That is why so many disagreements and emotional conversations with BP/NPs don't get resolved. The present situation is only the trigger for the BP/NP to feel exactly like he or she did in a past situation. These transferences don't make a lot of sense in the present moment. This is why the BP/NP may seem to be so overly sensitive and illogical.

STOP DISASTER-VISION

The other way that feelings get over the top occurs when your thoughts go to future fears of what might happen. Caretakers are too often overly focused on what will happen next. You may be continually looking out for the next disaster to happen. This gets in your way of handling things in the present and responding calmly. Typically, when you are looking into the future, you begin running dozens of disaster-vision scenarios: "He could take the children away if I . . . ," "She could have a meltdown at Thanksgiving if . . . ," or "He might not speak to me for days if . . ."

Do you see how this disaster-vision focuses on the BP/NP, what they might do, and how to manipulate them rather than on you and what decisions you want and need to make at the present time? Yes, your decisions will have an effect on the BP/NP, but looking totally at what the BP/NP might do doesn't lead you make to make good decisions.

Disaster-vision leads to lots of anxiety, uses up a tremendous amount of energy, and doesn't come up with real, workable solutions to the issues before you. There are better ways to problem solve and handle delicate situations with the BP/NP that we will cover in coming chapters.

GIVE UP HOPE, GIVE UP GUILT, GIVE UP SHAME

Another really important change in your attitude that is necessary is *giving up hope*. To let go of the Caretaker role, you will have to give up the hope that the BP/NP will ever change to please you, that the BP/NP will ever love you the way you want to be loved, or that the BP/NP will ever take care of you first. Giving up these unrealistic hopes will improve your health and well-being. It is part of the process of moving from fantasy to reality. If the BP/NP doesn't already do the things you have always hoped for on a regular basis, you need to realize that he or she never will. Interacting with the BP/NP in an effective way will have to come entirely from you, and you have to accept that this is the way things are. Your hope for a better relationship needs to be transferred from trying to heal the BP/NP to your own healing. Just as your life is your journey alone, so is that of the BP/NP. The BP/NP's healing is in his or her own hands, not yours.

Giving up guilt is also important. Many Caretakers feel bound up with the BP/NP through guilt. You have been responsible for the well-being of the BP/NP first and foremost, maybe for years or decades.

You have believed that the BP/NP will be hurt, feel rejected, attempt suicide, become deeply depressed, or fly into a rage all because of what you do and say. But haven't you seen the BP/NP do these things even when you were trying your level best to do exactly what the BP/NP wanted? Just as you can't change or stop the BP/NP's behavior, you also can't *cause* his or her behavior. Therefore, you are not responsible for the BP/NP's behavior or feelings. The BP/NP uses guilt to manipulate and keep you trapped in your own belief that you are essential to the BP/NP. This belief of your omnipotence in the BP/NP's life keeps you from facing the real struggles of the final stages of your own growing into adulthood—that is, responsibility for yourself.

You also have to *give up shame* so that you can love yourself enough to make the life you really want. You can't make good changes in your life, take better care of yourself, feel good about yourself, or allow yourself to be vulnerable with others unless you quit feeling shameful. Guilt comes from feeling that you have hurt another person or taken a wrong action. Shame is the result of feeling that you are worthless, that you are a mistake, or that there is simply something wrong with you as a person. You may find it difficult to identify your shame, so here are some examples:

You feel that no one will ever really love you.
You don't let people see your mistakes.
You don't like your body.
You hide your emotions.
You are afraid to disagree with someone you care about.
You don't stand up for yourself.
You are afraid that others will reject you.
You think that others are judging you.
You believe that you have to prove your worth to others.

Letting go of shame happens simultaneously as you learn to care for and value yourself. When you come to the decision that you are the real judge of your life and that you belong on this earth as much as anyone else, you will find that you no longer feel there is something wrong with you, and the BP/NP can no longer manipulate you with shame.

YOU REALLY NEED HELP FROM OTHERS

When you give up guilt and shame, you almost immediately recognize that you need help from other people. No one exists alone, and although your inner journey to health is your journey alone, many other people can support you and sustain you in this journey. In order to get that help, however, you will have to search it out and ask for it.

Find Role Models

If you know a really healthy person who is happy, fulfilled, good at relationships, and an excellent parent, adopt him or her. This may sound flippant, but I mean it quite seriously. Even in unhealthy families, there are usually *some* healthy people. Look at your extended family and friends to see if anyone qualifies to be a healthy role model for the kind of life you want to have. Look at friends and coworkers or acquaintances. Reach out to these healthy people and begin deeper relationships. Hang out with them, invite them into your life, or move more into their circle. Look, learn, and copy how they communicate and how they make decisions and treat others in relationships. You can move toward greater emotional health by having more healthy relationships and role models.

Watch Television

This may sound really ridiculous, but a television series with a character you can clearly identify as emotionally healthy or working to be healthy can be a great model for learning social interactions and problem-solving skills that you missed. I had a client who taped and watched *Friends* over and over to learn how people make and keep friends, forgive each other, accept flaws in others, and have fun. Movies and television programs that show people successfully facing life challenges, standing up for themselves, being honest and direct, and who are joyous and can have fun are good models for how to handle life. Shows that are emotionally lethal are ones with borderline or narcissistic characters who harm other people and get away with it or where people get rejected or demeaned or are blown up in the last 10 seconds with no hope of being saved or protected. Those shows can increase your anxiety, disaster-vision fears, and the transfer of feelings from the past that can slow down your progress.

Join a Group

Whenever we join a group, we automatically start using, feeling, re-creating, and behaving in the same patterns that we use daily in our personal relationships. It has been my experience that Caretakers hate most groups. This is often for good reason. While you are deeply into Caretaker behavior patterns, you will likely find yourself trying to take care of everyone in the group, something that obviously is exhausting and not worth going out of the house for. Or you may find there are other Caretakers or borderlines or narcissists in the group. This can trigger fear, hatred, disgust, or dependence in you, and this is naturally uncomfortable.

It is very important to select a healthy group. It can be a social group, one focused on your interests (e.g., hiking, crafts, or community service), or even a therapy group. Don't assume a group is healthy just because it is popular, is connected to a church or other social agency, has "selective" criteria, and so on. Make sure the group actually interests you and meets your needs. Ask people who are in the group why they like it, and ask people who left the group why they left. Initially, make sure the group has a moderator or leader that you like, admire, and respect. This will help you feel braver and safer when old emotional reactions and dysfunctional patterns appear either in you or in others. I recommend that groups, whether they are friends, coworkers, or professionals, become an important part of your lifestyle. Caring group members can stand in for the lack of healthy family members, and groups can be an arena for learning healthy interactions and emotional support over time.

Get into Therapy

You cannot do this healing alone. I cannot emphasize this enough. Caretakers are usually missing some very important experiences that are necessary to become a healthy person. If you are a child of a BP/NP as well as a spouse, you may not have a clear idea of what you don't know. Just being in a long-term relationship with a BP/NP means that you have missed out on a lot of validation, your social skills may have deteriorated, you may be confused from being blamed for everything by the BP/NP, your expectations of others may be too much or too little, you may be battling depression, or you may have anxiety that doesn't respond to typical treatment. Over time, Caretakers become easily manipulated and confused about reality, fantasy, and delusion. You may have become highly self-critical, and your self-care and self-respect may need support.

You deserve to get the caring, support, and validation that therapy can offer. You may also need the kind of objectivity and knowledge about mental illness that is more than you can get from your friends or books or from having time pass. Having a trained, experienced therapist who specifically understands the BP/NP can really help you sort things out. Not a lot of therapists have this kind of training or experience, so ask specifically what training, reading, and workshops the therapist has had.

Embracing new, more reality-based thoughts and behaviors can go a long way to reducing the stress and negativity in your life. Changing your focus from the BP/NP's life to your own life's goals and purposes can turn you in a new direction. You can move from away being a Caretaker to creating a happier, healthier life that fulfills your own dreams and goals.

Chapter Thirteen

Increasing Your Self-Confidence

One of the ways you may have felt stuck in this relationship with the BP/NP is a lack of self-confidence. Your feeling responsible and to blame for all that goes on in your relationship with the BP/NP can chip away at your sense of self-respect and self-esteem, and it can wear away your confidence in your own insights and intuition, making you feel powerless, selfish, hopeless, and depressed.

You have the insight and ability to develop skills that can make your life more enjoyable, happier, healthier, and more productive. Getting back your sense of self-respect and self-confidence is very important. In the previous chapter, we talked about the two things you have the power to change: your behaviors and your thoughts. Increasing your self-confidence happens by changing your thoughts and behaviors toward yourself and taking good care of yourself.

DON'T TAKE ANYTHING PERSONALLY

It is important when dealing with the BP/NP to not take anything that he or she says or does personally. The BP/NP is very prone to blaming you for everything he or she thinks, feels, and does, and you need to come to terms with the fact that the BP/NP is not a reliable person to identify reality. About 90 percent of the time, whatever the BP/NP says about you is a much more reliable statement about him or her. This is called *projection*.

The BP/NP uses projection to shift the blame for his or her own failings, feelings, and disappointments onto you. It is a way to disown his or her own awful feelings, and it is a way to control you. This works really well for the BP/NP but not for you. Your willingness to take the BP/NP's feelings to heart and worry about him or her takes the responsibility for those feelings off the BP/NP and transfers them to you. When the BP/NP accuses you unfairly you typically go into overdrive trying to show the BP/NP that you are really very considerate, accommodating, and caring by giving into whatever the BP/NP wants. When you take what the BP/NP says and does as meaning something about you, the Caretaker in you steps in and does all the work to take care of the BP/NP's needs, wants, and feelings and abandons the job of taking care of you. This has to stop.

You are *never* to blame for how the BP/NP thinks, feels, or acts, just as the BP/NP is never to blame for your behaviors. You must let go of taking the blame and personalizing the BP/NP's emotions if you are ever going to gain control over your self-esteem and increase your self-respect. As long as you are carrying responsibility for the BP/NP's emotions and feelings, you cannot see or feel yourself accurately.

RESPECT YOURSELF

Basically, self-respect means to *consider yourself being worthy of high regard.*[1] So the first step is to actually *consider yourself*, that is, to think of your own needs and be able to identify those needs. Some examples follow:

Taking good care of yourself
Knowing what you feel
Honoring your strengths
Understanding your shortcomings without self-blame
Thinking about what you want
Defining goals for yourself
Listening to your own preferences
Choosing your own friends
Acknowledging your needs
Protecting yourself

There are, of course, thousands of possibilities. What would be on your own list?

The second part of respecting yourself, is to see yourself as *worthy*. Being worthy means that you know your own merit and value and that you treat yourself and expect to be treated according to that value. Remember that if someone is treating you poorly and you are allowing it, you are agreeing with that person's estimate of your value.

How do you see your worth? Does your worth depend entirely on how others value you? How do you respond when some people see you as worthy and valuable and others do not? Which do you believe? The worth you see in yourself will be reflected in how you treat yourself and how you allow others to treat you.

Yes, you're right, you can't control how people treat you, but you can certainly influence their behaviors by setting standards about what you will allow and sticking to them. If you're being treated badly, you can speak up and tell the person what kind of treatment you want instead. You can leave the interaction. You can choose to be around people who treat you better. You can even choose to be alone rather than be subjected to the treatment the other person is handing out. You have a lot of choice in the matter. And your choice is the signal to the rest of the world about how you see your worth.

You really need to spend some time identifying where you see your sense of self-worth. A lot of Caretakers tell me they have high self-worth, but when they accept daily abuses and bad treatment, their assertion seems to represent where they want to be, not where they really are. See if this is happening to you.

The final part of our respect definition is the concept of *high regard*. The role of Caretaker includes a lot of behaviors that do not bring to mind the idea of high regard. For example, not considering your own feelings, needs, and wants when making choices; not taking care of your physical needs; and not even knowing what you like and don't like do not qualify as high regard. These behaviors give no regard to yourself whatsoever.

So let's say that high regard is a 10 and that no regard is a 0. Where are you in your current relationship with the BP/NP? Don't pick a number where you would like to be and don't pick a number where you think you ought to be or where you are at work. Pick a number that really represents the respect and value you feel in your relationship with the BP/NP. This is your current baseline. Now think of where you would like to be. This tells you how much ground you have to cover to bring your self-respect up to where you could make better choices and enjoy a better life.

So how do you go about improving your self-respect? Everything in this book is about improving your self-respect. However, the core to improving self-respect is to treat yourself in every good way possible. Your self-respect improves every time you do the following:

Listen to your feelings
Honor your own dreams
Love and care for yourself
Stop interactions that are hurtful to you
Eliminate negative self-put-downs
Take the time to think of what you want
Speak up for yourself
Believe the best about yourself
Hang around people who really like you just the way you are

Make your own list of things that improve how you feel about yourself. Keep it in a conspicuous place and add to it. These actions tell your inner sense of self that you love, honor, and respect yourself. When you feel high self-respect, you will automatically direct yourself to people who will treat you the same way.

Keep in mind that you have to respect yourself first before you can expect others to respect you. By setting the limits on what you will do and not do, you are setting the boundaries of your self-respect. Remember that everything that happens to you in your relationships is because you allowed it, encouraged it, or put up with it. When you set clear limits on how you will be treated, others see those limits and respond appropriately.

By establishing your own self-respect, preferences, and self-value, you will see a corresponding increase in your self-confidence. Self-respect means that you are going to stop merging with the BP/NP, and he or she may see this step of independence as a personal rejection. (In the next chapter, we will go over some ways to soothe and comfort the BP/NP while maintaining your own identity.) Whenever there is a merging of identities, someone's self-respect has been trampled on. In this relationship, that means yours. So stick to your own respectful view of yourself despite the BP/NP's anxiety.

Do you know what you value in life? Do you know why you have these values? Do you know such everyday things about yourself as how you like to dress, how you like to sleep, what and when you like to eat, and how much time you like to spend with others and how much time alone? Make sure you own what you are doing and know that these are your own choices. Only then will you experience a real respect for yourself.

START POSITIVE SELF-TALK AND POSITIVE ACTION

Another step in helping you feel stronger and more confident will be eliminating the negative things you say and feel about yourself, and then replacing them with positive self-talk. What would you like to be saying to yourself? What positives can you put into place instead of the negatives? You may not believe the positives yet, but even saying to yourself what positives you would *like* to feel begins creating better feelings about yourself.

Affirmations, which are positive statements you make about yourself and say over and over, can certainly help. However, all talk and no action doesn't get you very far. You have to take action to treat yourself more positively too. If you don't give yourself better treatment, your inner sense of self will not believe your positive statements.

Positive self-talk is a great way to show yourself respect. How do you talk to yourself in the privacy of your own mind? Do you talk to yourself like you would to a friend, a loved one, or the most valued person in your life? If you are not being positive toward yourself, why not? If you find yourself criticizing yourself, calling yourself names, deriding yourself, and even emotionally punishing yourself, why are you doing this? What is your goal? These internal negative self-attacks may seem automatic, but you can learn to control and redirect them toward positive self-support with practice and vigilance.

Research shows that validation and reward go much further in creating and inspiring positive change in self-esteem and behaviors than criticism and punishment. The following three-step system is very powerful in supporting positive self-change:

Step 1. Validation of what you have done well
Step 2. A gentle request to make a change of your choosing
Step 3. A statement of encouragement and confidence

For example, a client who wanted to stop constantly apologizing for everything said to herself, "Wow, I got through seven minutes of talking with Jill without apologizing at all. I did notice that I apologized for not eating fast enough, which I didn't need to do. I'm going to watch out for that one in the future. I know I can quit doing that one too."

Positive self-talk can also help you plan an interaction and encourage yourself about how you wish to act. You can decide ahead of time how you want to approach a conversation, deal with a confrontation, encourage more closeness, and so on. You can be a coach to yourself by encouraging yourself when you are feeling tentative and giving yourself validation when you get through a new experience. There is a lot of evidence that the more positively you talk to yourself, the higher your self-confidence becomes.

BALANCE YOUR EMOTIONS AND THOUGHTS

Balancing your emotions with thoughts may take some practice if you have been used to the over-the-top emotionality of a BP/NP-dominated relationship. The BP/NP focuses almost entirely on feelings rather than thinking. The BP/NP acts out, dwells on, and exaggerates feelings so that when you are around him or her, it can be difficult for you to think and make rational decisions.

It can even be hard to know what you are thinking when all around you are feelings of anxiety, fear, anger, and so on from the BP/NP. Learning to tune into your own thoughts and dial down your attention to the emotions in the interaction with the BP/NP can take some real concentration. Strong feelings can be triggered by a sound or smell, a voice inflection, or a touch, and they can then move through the nervous system a hundred times faster than thoughts. That is why habitual emotional reactions seem to happen even without thoughts.

So to be in more control over your emotional reactions, you will need to be aware of your thoughts and have them in place before you go into situations that have caused major emotional reactions in the past. This can be very helpful when interacting with the BP/NP who seems to be so able to easily "push your buttons."

Your emotional buttons are often the negative things you secretly think about yourself that you try to ignore or even pretend that you don't really think. For example, if you know you are rail thin and someone says you are fat, you probably just think they need their eyesight checked. But if you secretly believe that you are too heavy and someone says you're fat, you may find yourself feeling hurt or insulted. Your emotional reaction button gets pushed more easily when your self beliefs are in alignment with what the BP/NP says about you.

BP/NPs can make you extremely furious and hurt when they tap into your emotional buttons. You think the BP/NP is *making* you feel these bad things about yourself, but the BP/NP is actually tuning into the negative self-criticisms that you already have. Instead of just reacting, use these experiences to identify your emotional buttons and negative self-thoughts and work on healing them. When you identify negative self-beliefs and replace them with positive strengths and self-validations, you can begin turning off the emotional buttons that the BP/NP has used in the past to cause you hurt.

Try listing your most feared and upsetting self-thoughts. Common thoughts may include the following:

I'm not lovable.
I'm not good enough.
I'm too selfish.
I'm not good at . . .
I don't deserve . . .
I'm not worthwhile.
I'm useless.
It is all my fault.

As long as you believe these things about yourself, your self-confidence and belief in your value and goodness will be in jeopardy. Challenge these old negative self-criticisms using facts about your behaviors and character:

I deserve a vacation as much as anyone else.
I am a thoughtful and sincere person.
I am a good cook.
I am a caring parent.

Notice how you feel when you say positive things to yourself. Your self-respect and confidence increase. Prove to yourself how your emotions change depending on what you say to yourself and how you take care of yourself.

Balancing your emotions and thoughts can make a significant difference in your quality of life. Focusing only on emotions is one of the things that gets the BP/NP into so many crazy and upsetting situations. On the other hand, not giving any consideration to your feelings will also get you going in the wrong direction. You don't want to be a robot any more than you want to live as an emotional wreck.

Feelings are actually a combination of emotions and thoughts blended together. Raw emotion is really a physical reaction caused by a chemical release in the body. Feelings are the result of observing that emotion and making some kind of sense out of the reaction. Feelings are an essential component to coming to good decisions about what to do in specific situations. For example, the feeling of loving someone is one of the most complex we experience and includes many emotions and sensations (e.g., warmth, safety, excitement, and lust) and many thoughts (e.g., attractiveness, interests, and opinions), and these blend together to lead us to behaviors and choices that may affect us for the rest of our lives.

Look at the thoughts and meanings that you connect with various emotions, such as anger, hurt, joy, fear, and comfort. Explore the meanings, thoughts, and memories you have associated with these emotions as you confront new situations. This will lead you to a greater understanding of what you want and what you value. With this knowledge, you can make better decisions about what actions to take.

CONTROL YOUR OWN FEELINGS OF INTIMIDATION

The BP/NP is a master of intimidation. Because BP/NPs are totally focused on getting what they want and need to feel better, they are willing to threaten, cajole, demand, beg, and complain over and over until they are successful, all with very little thought for the effect on you. Recently, I heard from a client whose NP wife just ignores anything that she doesn't like. He said they were in a restaurant, and he was telling her that they had lost 40 percent of their savings in the stock market downturn. Her response was, "I just won't believe that. That can't possibly be true. You are just being mean to me." She then proceeded to order the most expensive item on the menu. I asked him what he did then. He paid for the meal, felt resentful, and gave in to her intimidation.

How are you being intimidated by your BP/NP partner, parent, or co-worker? Remember that whenever you suddenly start feeling anxious, guilty, or stupid around the BP/NP, you are being manipulated, so start looking for the intimidation. In order to get out of the intimidation cycle, you have to find a way to no longer cooperate with the goals of the BP/NP.

When you are told by the BP/NP that your ideas, wants, needs, and feelings are totally without merit, why do you believe this? You cannot be intimidated into giving up what you feel if you truly believe in yourself, your rights, your connection to reality, and your internal integrity. Does it make sense to you to let a mentally ill person be the judge of these things for you? When you become the final judge of who you are and what you will do, then you will set yourself free from intimidation by the BP/NP, and your anxiety will become more manageable.

LET GO OF YOUR DEPENDENCE ON THE BP/NP

Separating the control of your life from the BP/NP will help you create a life of your own that is relaxed, calm, and nurturing. BP/NPs keep control of you when they threaten to take away their love, money, fidelity, or commitment in the relationship with you. Do you seriously want to be emotionally and physically dependent on a person who is out of touch with reality, mentally ill, and often an emotional time bomb?

How dependent are you on the BP/NP? Does he or she provide all the income, the child care, your sense of well-being, or your social life? Your anxiety will always be high as long as you depend primarily on the BP/NP for anything. BP/NPs cannot be highly dependable because of their emotional ups and downs and their tendency to let you down just at the moment you need them to be there for you. Assess what dependencies you have on the BP/NP in your life and decide what to do about these. Do you need to get a job, get the children in daycare, find your own friends, or love yourself more? Whatever it is, now is a good time to start moving toward becoming more independent and, therefore, less anxious.

LEARN SELF-ASSERTION

The idea of being more assertive can feel very dangerous at first when dealing with a BP/NP. One of the skills that is often poorly developed in Caretakers is self-assertion. The BP/NP can be very clever at getting you to give up your desire to ask for or say what you want, so you are going to need to reclaim your sense of self by developing the skill of asserting your views and wants. Often Caretakers give up their own wants because BP/NPs react so angrily or override your ideas with what they want, or they conveniently forget or just plain ignore what you want. However, it is important to know and say what you want in your own life. Much of a person's identity is manifested in what they identify they want and what they are willing to stand up for and aim for.

However, if you focus on asking the BP/NP to change, to accommodate you, or to act differently, you will surely get nowhere most of the time. A more effective way of being assertive is to say what you think, what you feel, and what you want to do and then go do it yourself. Give up thinking that you can change the BP/NP's behavior by asking him or her to change. The way to create change in your life is to do it yourself.

Most Caretakers tell me they have already tried being assertive but that nothing has changed. If things have not changed, it is likely that you have been trying to get the BP/NP to change, and you have not been truly self-assertive in the way I'm talking about. Most Caretakers state their wants and goals cautiously and vaguely and imply that the BP/NP needs to change or do something about them. You rarely stand a chance trying to get what you want in this manner. Instead, try these steps:

Identify what you want.
State clearly what you think, feel, and want nonemotionally.
Don't discuss.
Decide what action you wish to take.
Take the action.

Focus on making statements about what you are going to do and on the actions that you can take:

Instead of	Say instead
I want you to be more affectionate.	I've decided I want more affection in my life.
I want you to be nicer to me.	I've decided to be nicer to myself.
Why can't you listen to me?	I want to be heard when I share my thoughts
Stop being so angry.	I've decided to not be around angry people.
Can I go back to school?	I want to finish my college education.

By stating what you want and plan to do without identifying the BP/NP as bad or as the problem or needing to change, you put a new idea out about who you are and what you are going to do, leaving the BP/NP to choose whether he or she will be part of the change.

Identifying to yourself what you want is essential to your sense of identity and self-esteem. Whether or not you can get what you want from the BP/NP, at least you have clarified for yourself the direction you want to take in your life. If the BP/NP doesn't want to or won't or can't respond to the change you would like, you still have the option to figure out how to make your life more of what you want with or without him or her.

Identifying what you want places you where you need to be, that is, as the director of your life. This also helps you see that the BP/NP does not control your life—you do. When you never say what you think, feel, or want, in all practicality you don't exist.

TRUST YOUR INTUITION

Your intuition becomes easier and more accurate when you are not enmeshed with the BP/NP. You cannot get a good sense of what is good for you when you are also carrying around the BP/NP's feelings and needs. Intuition is your inner sense of knowing what action will lead to the best result for your well-being. It involves being able to read other people's body language accurately, understand the meaning of what is going on, and know yourself well enough to accurately take actions that will lead to positive results for your life. Intuition develops and becomes automatic after you have practiced over and over knowing yourself and accurately knowing other people.

Caretakers often have a highly developed intuition for the BP/NP's feelings, wants, and needs, but you may not be as intuitive about your own. Enmeshment with the BP/NP makes it hard to tune into you own meanings about what is happening. You may have been automatically taking the BP/NP's meanings as your own, without thinking through what it really means to you. You may find yourself automatically believing what the BP/NP says about you without really deciding if that is true from your perspective.

As you let go of the enmeshment between yourself and the BP/NP, you will see both of you more accurately. You will begin to understand the BP/NP's true needs, fears, motivations, and anxieties better, and you will be able to see how they are different from your own. Intuition about yourself can lead you to a better sense of what you want and value and will make it easier for you to make better decisions about your own life direction.

TAKE CHARGE OF YOUR OWN LIFE

In order to move through the stages from Caretaker to self-care, you need to know what you think, how you feel, what you want, and how you want to live your life. As a Caretaker, none of these things is very clear because you are constantly tuning into the needs and emotions of the BP/NP rather than yourself.

When you move to caring for yourself, you will find that your self-confidence increases as well as your awareness of who you are and what you want in life. Your job in life is to live your life the way you choose. This is not selfish, uncaring, or disloyal, which is what the BP/NP may want you to believe. Being you is what you are here to do. Being in a relationship with another person is enjoyable, but it can't be done effectively and happily until you know who you are and what you want in your own life.

When you are caretaking the BP/NP you are not effectively taking care of yourself. You are not adequately being responsible for yourself because you are not even paying attention to what you are feeling and doing. It is your responsibility to be in charge of your own life, not the BP/NP's life. You are responsible for what you do, how you think and feel, and how you live your life. Being in charge of your own life means deciding who you are and what you want to do and taking responsibility to do it. . Now is the time to let the BP/NP take care of his or her life and for you to focus on yours.

Chapter Fourteen

Nurturing and Caring for Yourself

The task of giving up the Caretaker role will require that you be physically, mentally, and emotionally prepared to make some big changes. Up to now, you have been hoping that the BP/NP would get well and start taking care of you and your needs like you have been doing for him or her. Letting go of the Caretaker role means that you now recognize that you will be taking care of your own needs and wants and focusing less on the BP/NP. Learning to nurture and care for yourself is an important step in that change. Truly caring for yourself helps you to know yourself and your needs better and can help you get stronger and ready to challenge more effectively the emotional chaos of the BP/NP.

DIALING DOWN YOUR ANXIETY

Breathe calmly and continually. When you are angry, anxious, fearful, worried, and so on, you are probably not breathing very well. You may notice that you stop breathing for long periods of time, resulting in a sudden intake or exhale of breath. It can be helpful to notice whether you hold your breath with the air in or out of your chest. Then you can remind yourself, "Breathe in, breathe out" or "Let it go, let it go." Learning to control your breath can have a strong effect on your emotions and energy. For instance, holding your breath with the air out can make you feel vulnerable because you have little or no energy for action. Your brain begins to lose oxygen, and your thinking begins to deteriorate. Holding your breath with the air in helps you prepare for action, but often the action comes out too strongly and harshly, leading to negative escalation and hostility.

You might also notice yourself breathing fast and only in the top part of your chest. This kind of breathing will make you feel more anxious, so slow it down and breathe more deeply. If you find yourself taking deep, rapid breaths with a lot of breathing out, you will be triggering yourself to get angry. Notice what kind of breathing you are doing and take control of it to help yourself stay calm or prepare for action. Choosing how to breathe will also help you match it to the kind of action you decide to take.

Walking, swimming, singing, and dancing are all enjoyable ways to become more aware of your breathing. Notice over and over during the day how you are breathing. Spend some time each day practicing relaxation breathing to get your body used to breathing to your command. This ability to relax your physical body can help you relax your mind as well.

Getting lots of rest is extremely helpful in reducing anxiety. Living with a BP/NP is an exhausting experience. You are in a constant state of arousal and hypervigilance waiting for the next emotional explosion from the BP/NP. It can be very difficult to feel calm and truly relaxed when you are so on guard. So keep in mind that you may need more rest than people who are not in relationship with a BP/NP. Losing sleep or sleeping poorly because of anxiety, anger, frustration, and so on can take a big toll over the years, too. You may also find your sleep interrupted by an anxious or upset BP/NP who wakes you in the night demanding to have a full-blown, emotional "discussion" or wanting sex because he or she feels insecure or just from their tossing and turning. Getting a handle on your own sleeping is essential.

You need to have a truly restful place to sleep. And you need to get enough sleep. Assess your own needs on this. If your partner is keeping you from getting this primary human need met, consider what you can do to get this need met more effectively.

> Madeline and her husband were getting close to retirement. The last of their children had left home. She had come to therapy on her own because she said she felt a "wall" between herself and him. We worked for about a year. During that time, she identified a lot of narcissistic traits in him that seemed more evident since the kids were gone. She loved her husband, but she often got annoyed with his constant focus on himself and his never-ending need for her attention. Her parents had left her some money, so she began fixing up a garage on the back of their property into a little meditation house. She would do her art and meditation there. She found herself moving her free time more and more into the little house. During the summer, she put a bed in the place and started sleeping out there regularly. Instead of announcing to her husband that she was going to do this, she just did it. She said the result was that she got a lot more sleep, and she found that she liked her husband better. He said he was sleeping better too. They never discussed this change. She just did it.

Reduce stress around eating. Do you eat when you get stressed? Do you find it hard to eat anything when you're stressed? What kind of stress happens around the dinner table in your household? Look into these matters and find ways to eat where the emotions of the BP/NP aren't affecting everyone's digestion.For example,

> Andrea reported to me, "Dinner time at our house was fine unless my father was home. My BP mother was a good cook, so we had good meals. About three or four times a week, my father didn't get home from work till after dinner. On those nights, my mother hardly said a word, and my sisters and I got through dinner pretty well. Although I loved evenings when my father was home early, it was also an edgy time around the dinner table. We all talked more then, and somehow my mother would inevitably blow up about something. I was rail thin when I lived at home. And when I got married to another BP, I instituted the idea of eating dinner around the television. Sitting around the table either set me off gobbling my food or losing my appetite altogether."

Taking control of the basics of eating, sleeping, and free time is essential to reducing your anxiety.

CREATE A REGULAR ALONE PLACE

Your alone place can be any room or space where you can be alone. Basically, it needs to be a space where you can sit quietly and think or read a book or do anything you want. Madeline had the money to create a new space, but look around and see what is available to you. Your space needs to be one that discourages or limits the entry of the BP/NP. An extra bedroom room, a den or office, or even a space in the garage are all good possibilities. As a child, I sat in a tree in the backyard. I've also heard of people using a tent in the backyard, a closet, a neighbor's house, or a special place by a lake or river. Some people take a drive or a walk by themselves. Spending regular alone time is necessary to establish your right to be alone and to have the space to think your own thoughts.

One of my clients went to a workshop on centering prayer, came home, and set up the extra bedroom as a prayer room and went there regularly. Her NP husband, who thought that her actions were ridiculous, avoided her at all costs when she was in that room. She didn't even need to put a lock on the door to discourage him from coming in. You can start any activity that you love and that your partner doesn't enjoy and do it whenever you need to get away, such as sewing in your sewing room, woodworking in your garage, daily walks alone or with the dog, grooming the horses, meditating, or taking a two-hour bath—whatever works for you.

Being alone to think and focus on what you feel, need, and want in life is essential when you are in a relationship with a BP/NP. Having somewhere to go and something to do can help lower your anxiety and short-circuit your automatic response to engage with the BP/NP in useless, antagonistic, and inflammatory discussions or arguments that just make your relationship worse.

What I would greatly discourage, however, are addictive activities that do not help you think, relax, and take care of yourself. These would include shopping, watching hours of television, surfing the Internet and chat rooms, drinking alcohol, doing more than an hour of exercise a day (unless you are training for a marathon), overeating, or bitch sessions with friends. These activities are really *avoidance* techniques that neither make you feel better nor help you to make better choices in your life.

DO THINGS WITH YOUR OWN FRIENDS

Do things with other people without expecting your BP/NP partner to join you. BP/NPs really pressure Caretakers into thinking that you have to do everything with them. Too often, when the BP/NP doesn't want to do something that you want to do, the BP/NP's veto controls both of you. By making your own friends and activities, you can create a life of your own that increases your independence. Unless you actually fear that the BP/NP would physically harm or restrain you, it is probably your own anxiety at being away from the BP/NP or your anticipatory fear that the BP/NP will be angry that keeps you from taking these independent actions. Look inside at what is really keeping you from doing the things you want.

CREATE YOUR OWN HAPPINESS

If you are depending on the relationship with the BP/NP to make you feel better, you have found out by now that it is not likely to happen very often. Start looking around at all the things in your life that can and do make you happy, such as your children, work, hobbies, friendships, leisure activities, a beautiful day of good weather, animal companions, or community service. What are the things in life that make you feel grateful? Get in touch with your compassion for others who don't have as good a life as you have. Reach out and give to others. Engage with other people who could and would appreciate your attention, help, encouragement, and support. Your whole life does not have to be completely focused on the BP/NP. There are plenty of people and activities in the world to engage in, enjoy, and bring you happiness. It may seem that when your relationship with the BP/NP isn't in a good place, you don't have time or energy for these other things. But what if you reversed the order? Make activities and service with others be a priority in your happiness and then see if that helps your relationship with the BP/NP.

ME FIRST

It is not selfish to take care of yourself. Putting yourself first may be very hard for you, and you may not have many ideas about how to take care of yourself. When you have spent so long focused on the BP/NP, it can be a challenge to move your attention to yourself. You may not feel deserving of taking care of yourself, or you may not have many self-care skills. You may not think you have the time to care for yourself, or you may not know what feels good to you.

Putting yourself first is not about being selfish and developing a "me" attitude. This is a reminder that, unless you take care of your body and mind, you will not be strong enough to make the changes you are trying to make. If you are exhausted or depressed, have no time to yourself, and are constantly at the beck and call of someone else, you cannot move out of the Caretaker role. Taking care of yourself in a healthy way is a change that can help you become more fully who you want to be, a process of loving yourself first. Only then can you give to others without depleting yourself and feeling resentful.

Remember that no one else in the universe has been assigned to take care of you. As an adult, you now have the job, whether you like it or not, of taking care of yourself. If you don't care for yourself, you will become more and more needy, demanding, and eventually emotionally and/or physically ill. Since everyone else is out taking care of themselves, they probably don't notice and can only guess what you need to feel healthy and good about yourself. Your main job in life is to become more and more of who and what you are and, therefore, to make your unique contribution to the human race. Obviously, no one else can make the contribution you have within you to make, and you can't do your best if you aren't taking care of yourself.

So the first thing to do is get your mind in line with the idea that taking good care of yourself is very important. It is important not only to you but also to everyone who loves you. You deserve it, and you have to do it or else suffer the consequences.

You may find that you have to let go of your desire to have the BP/NP do the job of taking care of you, along with letting go of any anger at the BP/NP for so rarely stepping up. You have to give up the magical thinking that by taking care of the BP/NP, he or she will love you enough to take care of you. Maybe the BP/NP will be caring of you (sometimes when he or she feels like it or has extra time or there is an emergency), but haven't you learned by now to quit expecting the BP/NP to do what you want?

No one can take better care of you than you anyway. Only you have 24/7 access to how you feel, what you want, how you want it, how much you want, and exactly what you want.

MEDITATION, RELAXATION, AND EXERCISE

Time spent quietly with your own thoughts and without interruption is a really valuable way to take care of yourself. When you live with a BP/NP, your thoughts are often not your own. Taking time every day to tune into what you feel, want, and believe is important. Take time everyday for yourself and let go of your thoughts and worries for 20 minutes or so. Be with yourself. Pray, do yoga, or practice sitting and meditating away from the BP/NP. Tell the BP/NP what you are doing but don't let him or her stop you. The goal is to learn to significantly reduce the constant hypervigilance, worry, and anxiety that weigh you down. One client did this by dancing, another worked in her garden, and another said that cleaning closets worked pretty well.

Learning to relax is another challenge. One woman in our Caretakers' recovery group said it took her two years after she left her BP husband to finally be able to relax enough to concentrate on reading a book. It is often very difficult to relax around the BP/NP because you feel you have to be on guard for the next uproar. Find times and places away from home, with your own friends, or anywhere the BP/NP can't disrupt you. Claim some time for yourself.

Moving, whether walking, running, tennis, lifting weights, and so on, can help to wash the feelings of frustration and anger from your body and help you find a quiet space in your mind to be aware of what you feel and want. If you feel yourself falling into depression, a great way to feel better is to exercise enough to get your heart rate up so that your body will release some of your natural endorphins and rebalance your serotonin levels. Going to the gym, attending an exercise group, or walking regularly has the added benefit of carving this time out for yourself, and it may even be the source of making some new, healthy friends.

HEALTHY WAYS TO GET NURTURED

Caretakers often don't get enough nurturing. Although exercise is a good way to release tension out of the body, it is rarely nurturing. Getting a massage or a reflexology session can do wonders to help you relax and become more aware of how your body feels, where you store tension, and can relieve anxiety, depression, and even shame. Just getting your neck and shoulders massaged can help you feel that your life is less of a burden. Any kind of spa treatments, such as facials, mud baths, body wraps, or manicures or pedicures, help too. All of these focus on your body, your needs, and your health in a nurturing way.

Living with a BP/NP can create a lot of tension and stress and a greater need for nurturing. When you are just becoming aware of your need for nurturing, it can really feel the best to have someone else nurturing you. However, as a Caretaker, it is unlikely that you have been willing in the past to spend the time or money on your own "selfish" needs. Check in with yourself. If you feel exhausted, unappreciated, overwhelmed, and always giving, it is time *now* to start a nurturing program to fill your deficit. One great benefit is that you will feel more kind, gentle, loving, and caring to others as well as yourself.

MEDS COULD HELP

There are safe and effective medications that can help you deal with your depression and anxiety. Many Caretakers have a low-level anxiety much of the time. It may be that after you do all the things suggested here, you still feel a constant dread, depression, or anger that you have to override in order to take the actions you want to take. Talk to your therapist or see your doctor to discuss your situation candidly, describing your symptoms specifically. Do not downplay your symptoms (something that Caretakers have a strong tendency to do). Then work with your doctor to adjust the medications to the level that works for you.

If you find that certain situations with the BP/NP create a lot of anxiety, try taking a short-acting antianxiety medication to help you get through those events. These medications can help you see that you did well and felt good, and can set the stage for you to let go of your fears the next time. You may also find that when confronting the BP/NP, an antianxiety medication can help you reach the level of calm you need in order to stay focused, not get triggered into anger, and be able to tolerate the uncertainty of the results without caving in. However, many antianxiety medications can be addictive if you rely on them instead of also putting into action the suggestions made in this chapter. Work closely with your therapist and physician at all times with this option.

ENJOYING BEING YOU

When was the last time that you enjoyed just being who you are? Feeling your feelings, thinking your thoughts, and making your own choices are the elements of really enjoying being you. All sorts of feelings can appear when you become yourself. You may feel frightened at the responsibility (no one to blame) or giddy with the excitement of doing things you've always wanted to do. You may feel newly alive or finally feel that you are fitting into your skin. Revel in these feelings, work through them, and learn to know yourself.

Your life is yours to live, to direct, and to be in. Notice how others react to the real you. Changing from being a Caretaker can be like the metamorphosis from caterpillar to butterfly. When you break out of your old skin and take the risk of flying instead of creeping along, it can be invigorating.

GET A SUPPORT TEAM

Don't think that you have to tough out all these changes by yourself. Create a team, including yourself, your therapist, physician, and a couple of time-tested friends or family member, to keep tabs on your progress. Learn to trust their input and observations about the reality of your situation until you can trust your own judgment. This is your support team for change. Use them by being honest and open so that you can learn what it feels like to feel calm and safe and cared for by others. This will also give you a template for finding new and loving people to include in your life.

Letting go of anxiety and learning to nurture yourself can take awhile. Some things will help a lot and some less. It may take some experimentation and practice. Some Caretakers find that they have to pull themselves out of anxiety every few seconds at first, but as they practice and increase their self-nurturing, they find that they can maintain for longer and longer periods of time. As you find people and situations that are free from anxiety, create connections with them and increase this contact as much as possible. Building a calm and safe environment is essential for a happier, freer, more fulfilling life, and this investment in yourself can really pay off.

Chapter Fifteen

Anxiety-Reducing Skills
with the BP/NP

Being closely tied to a BP/NP increases your awareness that any event or action the BP/NP doesn't like or finds uncomfortable can be expanded into an emotional uproar. You have previously concluded that giving in to whatever the BP/NP wants is the only solution unless you want to face a very high emotional price. At the same time, whenever you give into the behavior of the BP/NP, you reinforce his or her emotional drama, and you lose out on what you want to do. These lose-lose situations cause anxiety, resentment, anger, hurt, and lowered self-esteem in you. The cost for this continuous giving in and giving up can lead you to blowing up at the BP/NP; taking these frustrations out on your children, friends, or coworkers; or even hiding them in unhealthy, self-attacking ways, such as negative self-criticism, drinking, depression, or thoughts of suicide. In other words, your giving in to whatever the BP/NP wants costs you your sense of self.

In order to take more control of any situation with a BP/NP, you need to know some specific skills. As a Caretaker, you have been trying to keep the BP/NP calm in order to reduce the anxiety and drama. It is unlikely that these tactics have worked other than on a random basis. Remember that trying to control anyone else doesn't really work. However, learning to understand and deal with the typical situations you get into with the BP/NP can be very helpful.

After working on the earlier suggestions to change your own mind-set, strengthen your self-esteem, and nurture and provide for you own emotional needs, your next step is to learn more effective skills to function in relationship with the BP/NP. These skills include ones that help lower the BP/NP's fear and anxiety and also skills that can create change in your interactions.

Dealing with anxiety is an essential skill to have when you live and work around BP/NPs because they carry a lot of anxiety within themselves that seems to get passed on to everyone around them. The BP/NP may also use threats and passive-aggressive behavior to increase anxiety in *you* to get what they want. As a Caretaker, you may feel a huge concern about the over-the-top anxiety you will have to deal with if you make any changes with the BP/NP, so working on doing things that help the BP/NP feel safe are a good way to begin.

UNDERSTANDING THE BP/NP'S VIEW OF THE WORLD

The BP/NP seems highly unpredictable, suddenly changing from one emotion to another, reversing behaviors, pulling you in, and then pushing you away. However, a lot of the BP/NP's unpredictability comes from your expecting the BP/NP to act "normal." Whenever you start thinking that the BP/NP will act the way *you* would act or the way most people would act in a certain situation, you have lost sight of the reality of the BP/NP's mental illness. Your attempts to change the needs and feelings of the BP/NP are part of what creates the uproar and unpredictability. Actually, their internal needs and feelings are fairly primitive and really don't change very much. Acknowledging these basic, unchangeable aspects of the BP/NP will help life become more predictable. The following is a list of basic BP/NP needs and feelings:

1. Everything that is not in the control of BP/NPs will make them anxious.
2. Whatever feelings BP/NPs are experiencing are absolute facts to them, and they believe that these feelings are caused by someone else.
3. There is only the present *moment*. The past and future are nonexistent.
4. Unlike mentally healthy people, the emotions of BP/NPs are often not caused by their thoughts. They have an emotion first, and then their minds try to think of reasons for having the feeling.
5. BP/NPs assume that you perceive, think, feel, and want exactly the same as they do. When they perceive a difference between the two of you, they feel threatened and will usually try to convince you to change.
6. Any change in *anything* will cause extreme anxiety in BP/NPs.
7. BP/NPs cannot tolerate your being emotionally close or your being apart from them in any way.
8. BP/NPs feel deeply inadequate, unloved, and undeserving of love. (Note: This feeling cannot be changed by you.)

9. The emotions of BP/NPs are indescribably intense, similar to those of an infant. Their total focus is—and always will be—on making themselves feel better.
10. If you are not completely focused on the BP/NP, they feel nonexistent.

You cannot change any of these 10 facts.

In terms of emotional development, BP/NPs are more similar to two-year-olds than to adults. They typically do not believe that anything or anyone in their world is permanent. Only the specific emotions that BP/NPs are having in the present moment are real. They often do not remember past emotions, thoughts, or behaviors, and they feel convinced that their present emotion will last forever.

So ask yourself, "Would I expect a two-year-old to keep promises or remember to do chores, or be alone for more than a few minutes, or understand how to act at a formal gathering, or wait for anything, or do something that he or she didn't want to do, or be at ease in new situations, or to go along with a change of plans?" Of course you wouldn't. Your expectation that the BP/NP will consistently be able to do these things adds to your feeling that the BP/NP is unpredictable.

How do you get a two-year-old to feel comfortable, to do as you ask, to feel reassured, or to cooperate? The confusing difference is that this two-year-old is in an adult body and has adult intelligence and even much of the time acts like an adult. Only the BP/NP's emotional reactions and reasoning are at the two-year-old level. Obviously, you can't spank BP/NPs or pick them up and remove them from the situation or order them around—things you sometimes see adults do with children. However, there are a lot of things that you can do to make things work more smoothly. A lot of what good parents of two-year-olds have to do is maneuver to lower the child's anxiety level. This, too, needs to be done with the BP/NPs to help facilitate more positive interactions.

BE PREDICTABLE

Establish routines and don't change plans without a lot of advance warning to the BP/NP. Don't expect the BP/NP to adjust to changes that happen suddenly. One of my clients said that her BP husband needed anywhere from two to six weeks of notice for inviting guests over. Changes in daily routines may need to be brought up and discussed for several days or weeks before a change can be made. And it is totally useless to expect that the BP/NP will just step in and help when you are late or feeling tired. In situations where sudden changes must be made, the BP/NP will usually be anxious and angry that things aren't happening as usual, so expect him or her to be upset and uncooperative. Try to have a schedule for everything that you can.

GO *VERY* SLOWLY, STEP BY STEP

When bringing up a change, the following steps will really help:

Step 1: Drop a casual comment that is fairly general, such as," I hear that next semester I might be teaching an evening class."

Step 2: A couple of weeks or even months before the change, you could add, "I'm thinking that Monday or Wednesday might work for an evening class." Ignore any comments from the BP/NP and don't get into a discussion.

Step 3: At least a week later, ask, "Do you think I should teach the Monday or the Wednesday class?" Again, don't get into a discussion. Just acknowledge the BP/NP's preference and don't make promises to comply.

Step 4: When you actually know what night you will be teaching, say, "My department chair says I have to teach the Monday class. I know this will be hard for you. How can I make it easier for you?"

Step 5: Listen to the BP/NP's comments, complaints, and upset without getting involved yourself. Just acknowledge what a problem this is going to be for the BP/NP: "I can hear that this will be very difficult for you" or "I'm sorry this will be inconvenient for you." Do not expect the BP/NP to do anything special to accommodate you.

Step 6: Identify a couple of benefits for the BP/NP that will be appealing, such as, "That means you can watch *Monday Night Football* as loud as you want" or "Maybe your brother will want to come over and watch with you."

Step 7: Be prepared to wait days or weeks for the BP/NP to calm down. After that, it will be likely that the BP/NP will feel that you always teach on Mondays.

You may be saying to yourself that this is a lot of work. Yes, it is. However, it is very likely to work with considerably less emotional upset than what you have been doing. This could be compared to the steps you might take to ease a reluctant first grader into the idea of going to school for the first time. It reduces resistance and anxiety for the BP/NP and makes for less frustration and anger for you.

USE DISTRACTION

If you need or want to be gone for an activity, suggest something for the BP/NP to do that he or she really enjoys that will distract from your absence. Another variation of this is to plan your away activities when the BP/NP is happily engrossed in a regular activity, such as a weekly television show, before the BP/NP gets up or after he or she has gone to bed, while he or she is at work, or on the BP/NP's regular bowling night.

You may be thinking that you "shouldn't" have to do this kind of planning around the BP/NP. But why not? You would do this for your children or for a loved one who needs other kinds of special care. The high-anxiety reactions of the BP/NP happen when you forget that he or she is mentally ill and didn't plan for his or her needs.

If you're gotten embroiled in an argument or other hostile interaction that seems to be going nowhere, try quiet distractions. Excuse yourself to go to the bathroom, close the door, and stay there for 10 to 20 minutes. Suddenly remember that you have to go to the store immediately for something and be gone 20 to 40 minutes. Pick up a briefcase and let the BP/NP know that you would love to keep discussing this but that you have paperwork to get done before work in the morning. Work for at least a half hour. Have a friend on speed dial so that when you call him or her with the message 911, the friend will call you, and you can stop the argument with the BP/NP to answer the phone, walk outside, and talk for 20 minutes. These "time-outs" distract the BP/NP from the interaction and give him or her time to calm down and get out of his or her crazy thought pattern.

REFLECT THE BP/NP'S FEELINGS

Reflecting how the BP/NP feels is very helpful in soothing the BP/NP. By stating out loud and specifically what the BP/NP feels, you are showing the BP/NP that you really are hearing him or her. This has a calming effect. Just saying, "I understand," however, doesn't convince the BP/NP that you hear him or her. Specifically, identify the feeling:

I see that you are feeling really disappointed.
I'm sorry you feel so sad about this.
It sounds like you don't like the fried chicken.
You look angry and hurt.
I can hear how frustrated you are.

This is a way for you to let the BP/NP know you hear what he or she is saying without judgment. This helps the BP/NP remain calm and keeps you from getting pulled into an argument. At the same time, you are not giving up your point of view. You simply aren't stating any disagreement at this time.

DON'T OVERTLY DISAGREE

The BP/NP does not usually do well in the presence of the words *no*, *but*, and *you're wrong*. Since the BP/NP is always expecting to be discounted, rejected, or told that he or she is wrong, avoiding these words helps you avoid emotional explosions. Choosing your words carefully and exactly may seem silly or inconvenient, but it makes a big difference in the outcome.

When you have a different point of view that you need or want to express to the BP/NP, you can begin by stating what feeling or thought you heard from the BP/NP. Then add your views, wants, or needs tied together with the word *and*. As much as possible, avoid the word *but*:

> I know that you don't want me to go to the meeting tonight, *and*, unfortunately, I really have to go.
> I understand that you like the red blouse, *and* I like the blue one.
> I can hear that you are really disappointed that I can't go. Can we get together later for coffee?
> I see you are angry with Tommy about his grades. I also want to point out that he did bring up the C to a B this quarter.

By avoiding overt disagreement, the BP/NP feels more relaxed and calm and may be more able to hear a differing point of view. Keep in mind that telling the BP/NP that he or she is wrong will guarantee a fight, while adding additional information is more likely to encourage a discussion.

CREATE REGULAR COUPLE ACTIVITIES

When the BP/NP can count on a regular, enjoyable activity with you, he or she feels better about you and the relationship. Doing things together is more validating to the BP/NP than words. Figure out something that both you and the BP/NP like and make it part of your routine. Then when the BP/NP says that you "never do anything together," you can identify the regular activity and say how much it means to you and how much you enjoy doing it with him or her. The BP/NP often doesn't remember the past (especially past emotions), so this reminds the BP/NP of a positive event and the feelings that went with it. This is soothing and reassuring to the BP/NP and enjoyable for you as well. This helps the BP/NP feel valued by you, lowers his or her anxiety, and provides a balance for times when you want to do things alone.

SUMMARY

These skills may seem like they are placating or appeasing the BP/NP and therefore are actually caretaking skills. Caretaking skills, however, are aimed at keeping the status quo rather than making changes in the relationship. The skills and techniques in this chapter are designed to create a calm, validating, and emotionally aware atmosphere that provides a base for the change-creating skills in the next chapter.

In order to work effectively, you must apply these skills with confidence, and you need to be in control of your emotions. BP/NPs read your emotional responses even more closely than your words or behaviors, so having developed the emotional strength to not be intimidated by the BP/NP will be a big plus when following these suggestions.

Chapter Sixteen

Change-Creating Skills with the BP/NP

While the techniques in the previous chapter are designed to lower the anxiety of the BP/NP so that your interactions with him or her are more pleasant and relaxed, the skills identified in this section are aimed at making changes that you want to implement in your relationship with the BP/NP. These changes can help you protect yourself and help you start moving out of the Caretaker role. They can reduce the amount of negative interactions you have with the BP/NP, and they can improve your self-esteem and your quality of life.

Since BP/NPs do not like any kind of change that is not initiated by themselves, these skills will trigger resistance and create emotional uproar in the BP/NP. Using these skills will be the beginning of your truly stepping out of the Caretaker role, which the BP/NP will not like. So you need to be clear about what changes you want to make and be prepared to follow through. You have a right to have a better life. You have a right to your own feelings. You have a right to decide for yourself what you will and won't do. The more clear you are about the changes you want, the more likely you will be successful.

The following skills will work with anyone who is trying to control you, manipulate you, or in some way define you and run your life for his or her own benefit rather than yours.

SET BOUNDARIES AND LIMITS

Just as you need to set boundaries to keep your two-year-old from creating harm to him- or herself and others, so too do you need to set boundaries and limits on the harmful behaviors of the BP/NP in your relationship. First, you will need to identify when and how the BP/NP is trying to control and dominate your life, or trying to manipulate you into doing things you don't want to do, or trying to tell you how to think and feel. These are all violations of your right to be you, and they do not actually benefit the BP/NP. Then you have to decide what you want to do to stop the BP/NP's behavior from harming you.

Setting limits and boundaries on what you will allow, accept, and encourage the BP/NP to do to you is essential. A boundary is a line that you don't allow others to cross. You may think you are setting a boundary when you say, "I'm done, I'm fed up, I won't tolerate this anymore," yet too often in the past you have actually done nothing to change these things that you can't tolerate. Identify the boundaries that you want to protect and defend, then take real and effective steps to figure out what actions you are going to take to make that boundary stick.

Since the BP/NP strongly resists any boundaries, be prepared for an initial battle. However, if you make the boundary clear and firm and never ever give in, the BP/NP will eventually become accustomed to it and will relax. Usually, Caretakers are so afraid of the BP/NP's initial outburst or their threats of anger and hostility that you give in and lose all the gains made by identifying the boundary in the first place. Since this will be a challenge to both you and the BP/NP, choose your boundaries and limits carefully and sparingly.

Keep in mind that you cannot enforce a boundary or limit that you have no power over. You hold power primarily over what *you* will do if the boundary is breached. It is also helpful to set limits only about the things that are really important enough to warrant the amount of energy and emotional strength that it will require you to follow through.

You don't need to tell the BP/NP why you have made the boundary—just keep stating the boundary over and over and be sure to act on it consistently. Here are some examples:

> I am not okay with your yelling at me like that. If you can calm your voice down, I will listen; otherwise, I will leave the room.
> I told you that I need you to stop criticizing me. Since you can't stop criticizing and yelling, I'm going into my room for awhile.
> I have felt resentful when I loaned you money in the past. This is now the last money I will give you. From now on, I expect you to take care of these money problems on your own.

These examples include a statement about how you feel, what you want, and what you are going to do next. The examples also include a grace period that gives the BP/NP time to change his or her behavior and tells him or her what can be done to regain the interaction with you and be successful. When you set limits on negative interactions and reinforce positive ones, the BP/NP can learn how to get what he or she wants in ways that work better for both of you. However, don't expect the BP/NP to learn quickly. It may take months of absolutely consistent follow-through on your part to see a small change in the BP/NP.

TAKE ACTION, NOT DISCUSSION

Anything that you want to change will have a better chance of success if you simply change what you are doing. Taking action instead of discussing what you plan to do with the BP/NP gives you a greater chance of success. Action means that you either start a new behavior or quit doing something that you usually do. The thing to keep in mind is that you need to be able to control these behaviors entirely on your own.

For example, a client of mine has a narcissist wife who is always demanding and shouting that she wants him to listen to her. After many instances of his saying that he couldn't listen if she was shouting, he simply sat quietly, looked at her kindly, and just listened, not saying anything at all. When she was done, he told her what he had heard her say and asked her if he had heard her correctly. She was so shocked that she couldn't think of anything to say, and then she walked off.

Too often, Caretakers try to convince the BP/NP with words and logic to agree to the new change in behavior. You don't need the BP/NP's permission or agreement before you change your own behavior to something that works better for you. Actions are more believable and have more impact than words. If you want space, go take it. Don't argue with the BP/NP that you deserve to take it. Tell the BP/NP what you will or will not be doing and then just do it. Leaving a written message can even avoid the temptation to discuss the issue. But be reliable.

One of my clients with a very unsociable borderline wife was getting more and more upset that he could never go to any social events because his wife would never want to go with him. He would try to convince her that it would be comfortable and enjoyable, but even when she agreed, she would back out at the last moment. He was getting more and more angry, and I asked him who had control of whether he went. He said that she did. I asked him how she controlled whether he walked out of the house and went to the party or school event or whatever. He reluctantly agreed that she really couldn't, but then he was afraid she would be mad when he came home. I said, "So what? What will she do?" He said she might not talk to him for a few days. Again, I asked him if that was so bad that it was worth missing the event he wanted to go to.

He had already been dealing with this issue for years, so he was ready to take a chance on what would happen. When the next school event came up, he just told his wife that he was going to the meeting, got his jacket, and left. When he came home, he found his wife asleep in bed. The next morning, she didn't even mention it. So he started going to school events regularly, even the more

social ones. Then one day, he told her that he was going to the local bar and
grill to watch *Monday Night Football* and invited her. She, of course, said no,
and he simply left it at that and went off himself. When he came home that
time, she accused him of having an affair. He quietly stated where he had been
and left the room.

This way, he moved slowly back into a more social life for himself, even
though his wife wouldn't join him and didn't really like what he was doing.
He stayed calm and continued doing what he had decided to do.

Your BP/NP partner might complain that you are gone too much, that you
don't love him or her anymore, that you are being mean or selfish, and so on,
so it is very important that you have solidly established your confidence and
esteem and let go of thinking that the BP/NP's words and thoughts mean
anything about you. The BP/NP's anger and accusations will be less intimi-
dating when you know that it is only his or her mental illness talking and
really isn't about you.

The important thing to do is not to argue or even discuss. Simply state
what you have chosen to do and then reflect what the BP/NP feels:

> I like going to watch the football game at the Sports Grill, and I know you
> don't enjoy the games.
> I'm sorry you don't want to go to the PTA meeting tonight. I think it's
> important, so I'm going to go.
> I'm not having an affair. I love you, and I am going to dinner with my
> sister tonight.

Then take your action.

BE FIRM AND ALSO REASSURE

Being firm means that you stick to what you have decided to do differently,
even if by the time you get out of the house to do it, you don't really have the
interest or energy anymore. Wearing you down is one way the BP/NP discourages you from doing what you want. The BP/NP can throw chores or
tasks or various restrictions as well as tantrums, hysteria, and offers of sex at
you to get you to change your mind. The minute you give up, however, you
have to start from the beginning to reset the boundary. So it is extremely
important to get through the door, into your sanctuary, or out of the house
whether you actually feel like doing what you were going to do or not
anymore. Stay away until you reach the time that you told the BP/NP you
would return and then reliably and on time return to the BP/NP. This is the
same method that parents use to teach a very young child to tolerate their
absence.

Identifying a return time is very helpful in calming to BP/NPs. It identifies how long he or she has to take care of his or her own fears and needs. Giving a reassuring comment as you go can also help, such as the following:

I'll be at the meeting until 9 pm. I really look forward to having some time with you when I get back.

I love you very much, and I appreciate your being comfortable with my spending time with my friends.

We had such a good time today, and I'd really like to do that again. I'll see you in an hour after my meditation time.

Reassuring BP/NPs that you care for them and enjoy being with them, or reminding them of the good times you've had together helps them remember their connection to you and hold on to the good feeling while you are absent. The borderline is still likely to get hurt, angry, or emotional as you depart, while the narcissist is more likely to try to lure you to stay with him or her using sex, suggesting something "more fun" to do, or threatening abandonment. Don't buy into these emotional manipulations. Continue to be pleasant and loving and remind the BP/NP of when you'll be back and then be sure to go.

Just as parents of toddlers do, you can help the BP/NP adjust to your absences by having predictable leavings and returning, usually short times at first and then slowly extending them. You might also leave a "transitional object" with the BP/NP to remind him or her of your love. But instead of the stuffed animal, blanket, or pillow that you might leave for a young child, you can leave loving words as reminders to the BP/NP of your love, times you've shared together, and times you look forward to being with him or her. This is a more adult way of reminding the BP/NP that he or she is not alone and abandoned.

IGNORE PROVOCATIVE BEHAVIOR FROM THE BP/NP

Although you may find it very hard to disappoint or upset the BP/NP, keep in mind that the rules of positive reinforcement apply to every interaction with the BP/NP. The more you give in, the more BP/NPs escalate their behavior because you are rewarding them for acting badly. Paying any sort of attention to their emotionally provocative behavior is encouraging to them. Even your "punishment" is rewarding, such as demanding that the BP/NP stop what he or she is doing, shouting, threatening, or getting upset yourself. These are all ways that the BP/NP knows that he or she has your attention and is in control. Ignoring the sarcastic, angry, or belittling remarks of the BP/NP or his or her emotional acting out is important to reducing that behavior in the BP/NP.

But beware that it can be very damaging to your own well-being to sit there and take it all in, so practice all of the skills for increasing your self-confidence and nurturing yourself so that you can be strong enough to resist emotionally absorbing the BP/NP's threatening and angry remarks. Probably the best way to ignore the overly dramatic and hostile behaviors of the BP/NP is to exit and not be there at all. It works best to not make a production of leaving by shouting or throwing your own bad comments out. Instead, use the distracting and disappearing techniques that we discussed earlier. Suddenly "remember" that you have something to pick up at the store, that you need to take a nap, or that you need to mow the lawn. These actions convey the message that you won't participate, and they change the situation without creating more escalation.

BE CALM AND FRIENDLY AND QUIT DISCUSSING THE BP/NP'S REACTIONS

Do not discuss any uproar situation afterward. As a Caretaker, you may be a big supporter of the idea that you should talk out situations to make them better. This *does not work* with the BP/NP. BP/NPs are often very willing to talk about things and may bring up discussions themselves. But ask yourself whether you ever successfully talked things through with the BP/NP and had anything really change. My guess is rarely or never. Usually these talks just escalate into another emotional uproar. It is another way for the BP/NP to hang on to your attention in a negative way, and it pulls you into being the persecutor, complaining and demanding but with nobody feeling or acting any better.

So avoid trying to discuss past, present, or future situations. Remember that the BP/NP really relates only to *action* in the *present moment*, and if the present moment is going well, keep it that way. However, if the present moment is *not* going well, decide what you need to do and just do it. Emotional discussions don't solve things with the BP/NP. When the BP/NP wants to discuss a situation, simply smile, be calm, and, in a friendly voice, just say, "I'm busy right now" or "Now is not a really good time." The only time for serious conflict discussions with a BP/NP is with a trained intermediary, such as a therapist, mediator, or judge.

However, don't trick yourself into forgetting the situation. This same situation is sure to happen again and again, so spend some of your alone time, thinking over what *you* feel and what you plan to do the next time it happens and even brainstorm ideas about how to eliminate the situation if possible.

HAVE A PLAN BEFORE YOU DISCUSS

Think things over before engaging the BP/NP. Take time out to think before negotiating anything with the BP/NP. If the BP/NP comes to you to initiate a discussion, a decision, or anything that takes a calm, thoughtful response from you, be sure that you are completely ready. Taking time to think about things before engaging with the BP/NP will nearly always be to your advantage. The BP/NP will most likely be very adamant about solving things *now*, but don't get tricked into responding until you are ready and have your own plan.

When the BP/NP initiates a "discussion," you can predict that he or she is already in an emotionally negative space. Obviously, this means that it would not be a good time to discuss things. Instead of discussing the issue right then, say to the BP/NP, "Obviously what you are bringing up is important, and I need to give it some serious consideration. I'm going to really think about this. Let's sit down to talk about it tomorrow night." Then walk away and become unavailable.

Pick a later time when both you and the BP/NP can be in a calm state of mind. Then wait for the BP/NP to bring up the subject again. By creating some time to think through what you feel and want, you will be prepared for a calm discussion, and you can have a plan of action prepared. But don't be surprised if the BP/NP never brings up the discussion again. Just by putting the discussion off until later, many times the BP/NP will forget what was so important, and it will just work itself out by the actions you take.

USE REPETITION

When the BP/NP becomes persistent and demanding, one of the best ways to stop an argument is to make statements of what you want or don't want over and over again and then, as soon as possible, exit the interaction. Some examples follow:

I do not want to talk about this now.
I am going to the party at Sarah's.
I do not want to make a list of criticisms of you.
I am taking the children to school at 8:00.
I am leaving for work in five minutes.

The more you state over and over what you want or what you are going to do, the better you will be able to avoid getting into discussions and arguments with the BP/NP about things that aren't going to be solved by talking anyway. This repetition also helps the BP/NP get familiar with the idea that you are not going to engage in chaos, uproar, and drama. It is important to say your statement in as few words possible, in a soft and kind voice, and then back it up with your actions.

SUMMARY

The suggestions above demonstrate ways to improve your interactions with the BP/NP. This is not the same as trying to change the BP/NP or trying to convince him or her that you are right, nor is it a way of trying to make the BP/NP act nicer or give you more freedom. Instead, these techniques and skills, *which are all under your own control*, do not need the BP/NP to agree in order to effect change.

By deciding just what *you* will be doing and then taking action yourself, you stop caretaking the BP/NP and start taking charge of your own life. Instead of trying to please or appease or control the BP/NP, you are selecting and taking actions that can move *you* forward into a healthier and more enjoyable life without causing harm to the BP/NP or to yourself. It is not a placating action but rather a proactive behavior to make your life work better.

Using these techniques and skills will make your interactions with the BP/NP work more effectively, but they won't change the fact that you are in a relationship with a mentally ill and emotionally dysfunctional person. By behaving more rationally, by not buying into the delusion that things are okay, and by opting out of the dysfunctional patterns of communication and emotional volatility, you will begin to see your relationship with the BP/NP in a more factual, transparent light. You will be able to see more clearly what impact these interactions are having on you, your children, and your life. And you will see more and more clearly how your acting as Caretaker has kept the dysfunctional interactions going.

Chapter Seventeen

Leaving or Staying

When you realize what it takes on your part to live with a BP/NP, you may feel exhausted or overwhelmed. The BP/NP is rarely able to make changes in his or her thinking, feelings, and actions, so you will be the one making the changes, taking up the slack, and, in many ways, acting as a live-in therapist. The BP/NP will continue being who he or she is, and you will need to continue making adjustment to deal with his or her actions.

Will you be able to stay out of the Caretaker role? Will you be able to live a life that is happy and fulfilling for you? There are many issues involved in whether you decide to leave the relationship or whether you decide to stay now that you know the reality of your situation. Deciding how much contact to have can bring up some powerful issues about loyalty, self-respect, obligations, connections, and losses.

Some of the issues that you need to consider include the following: Is this a short-term or a long-term relationship? Are you related to the BP/NP (e.g., parent, child, or sibling)? Do you have children together? What are their ages, and how does the BP/NP's behavior affect them? How much enjoyment does this relationship bring you compared to the bad periods? What do your finances look like with and without the BP/NP? How well have the suggestions in this book worked out when you tried them? How much separation can you live with? Are there other issues to consider, such as drug or alcohol addiction; physical, emotional, or sexual abuse; and whether the BP/NP has other psychological or physical illnesses?

The frequency of symptoms of borderline personality disorder and narcissistic personality disorder can vary from numerous times a day to a few times a year, and the intensity of their behaviors can also vary. How much time do you spend dealing with these symptoms? How disruptive are they? And how enjoyable is the relationship when the symptoms are not present? These are all factors in how much contact you may want with the BP/NP.

If you have tried the suggestions in the earlier chapters and found them helpful in balancing the relationship, you may have found greater satisfaction in your relationship with the BP/NP, and you may find that continuing the relationship with the BP/NP can work fairly well for everyone. Or perhaps reading this book and evaluating your situation has clarified for you that you need to end or drastically change your relationship with the BP/NP.

NARCISSISTIC RELATIONSHIPS

Staying with the Narcissist

Many NPs are charming, funny, creative, energetic, and financially success-ful. They need a lot of attention and adoration, but that may be just fine with you, especially if you find that you enjoy giving that kind of attention. If you can maintain power over your own life and choices, and if the NP is not too domineering, demanding, or controlling, you may be satisfied with your life. Respectful behavior between you and the NP can help the relationship func-tion in a healthy way for the whole family. If you can accept that the NP is prone to overworking; seeks a lot of attention from others; focuses almost entirely on only his or her needs, wants, and feelings; and must to be in control of the money, then you may be able to figure out a viable relationship arrangement.

If you are able to use your power to get your needs and the children's needs met, if you and the NP have a solid commitment to staying together, and if you enjoy the personality of the NP, you may find that it is worth the effort you must make to keep things calm and functioning.

However, it is likely that you will do more than your share of the work of caring for the family, such as parenting, planning and scheduling, tending sick children, and dealing with emergencies on your own. If you are lucky, you will have an NP spouse who can validate your efforts, who acts charm-ing toward you most of the time, and who makes a good financial contribu-tion to the family.

It is unlikely you will get much credit from the NP or anyone else for all this extra effort because the NP tends to get the credit for how productive, friendly, and helpful he or she is in the community and at work, while your efforts behind the scenes may go unnoticed. If you can find ways to avoid being resentful of this imbalance in attention and recognition and if you are good at being able to give yourself credit and have a strong support system of friends, then you have a better chance of making things work out. Being able to appreciate what the NP offers the family will also be important to your happiness in this relationship.

If you are female, you may find it more difficult to appreciate the NP husband who hasn't been successful in the work world. We still live in a world that forgives people for being obnoxious and hurtful if they make a lot of money. But if the NP in your relationship is not making much of a financial, social, or emotional contribution, then you may question the value of the relationship more.

Years ago, I worked with a couple who appeared to outsiders to be out of balance in their contributions to the relationship.

David, an NP husband and Georgia, a Caretaker wife, had been married for 15 years. During the first 10 years of their marriage, they traveled all over the world with the Peace Corps and other volunteer organizations. David was outgoing and idealistic, found it easy to make friends, and was highly adaptable. However, Georgia, was shy, quiet, and somewhat anxious in social situations. She was happy to follow David around through all their adventures. When she brought up the idea of having children, the couple found that they were worlds apart in their ideas of how to live their lives. They spent five years discussing whether to have children and tried to settle down.

Georgia found a job with a national corporation and began moving up the ladder to vice president. David, who had a major in geography, found it hard to get a job teaching. He didn't like being tied down, creating lesson plans, or having to do the same thing everyday. He finally got interested in a volunteer civic project concerning factory chemicals leaking into the city's water. He had great plans to sue the city and the state and maybe even take it to the Supreme Court. He went to a lot of meetings, usually with stay-at-home moms. When he had an affair, the couple came in for counseling.

Georgia was hurt and angry. David said that it didn't mean anything and that he still loved her. They spent three years in counseling, and Georgia nearly did leave. However, both Georgia and David really enjoyed each other's company, and they decided to stay together. A year later, they had a daughter. David continued to stay at home working on his "projects," and Georgia, who loved her job, kept working.

Georgia came in a few times over the next five years to discuss her feelings about doing most of the parenting and housekeeping and holding down her job, but she could never really see herself being without David. She decided her life would just feel too sterile and empty without David.

I have learned over the years that I can only guess what really keeps people in particular relationships. When I first met the couple above, I would have bet that Georgia would leave. But there were elements in the relationship that were deeply important to Georgia that made it worthwhile for her to stay.

Leaving the Narcissist

Here is where the intensity of the NP symptoms and their frequency can make a big difference. When the NP has such strong symptoms that he or she cannot and will not consider your feelings, rights, and needs, you will more likely think that you have little to gain from continuing in the relationship. If the NP is a bully, rude, or rejecting or just cannot fathom how you could be different from him or her in any way, then it may not be worth your self-esteem to stay. I would recommend finding a way to leave if the NP is emotionally or physically abusive. The impact of abuse on you and your children can have a life-long impact. However, only you can determine what is best for you. For example:

> Laureen had been a stay-at-home mom and felt she couldn't leave her NP husband, Jerry, because at age 63 she believed she could not find a way to support herself, and she had tremendous guilt leaving her husband of 40 years who had had a stroke. Until Jerry retired, they had had a very good life. Yes, she had taken full responsibility for raising the children and doing everything that anyone in the family needed her to do. Her NP husband was a very high powered executive, and they lived very well financially.
>
> But when he retired, Jerry came home to run her life. He would yell and reprimand her and sometimes threaten her with his fist when something wasn't to his liking. After the stroke, he demanded that she be with him every minute of every day. She came to the Caretakers' support group, nearly ready to leave him. However, after learning ways to create a life for herself, she decided to stay.
>
> Laureen called a year later saying that her husband had died from a second stroke. She was glad she had stayed because it was "the right thing to do," but she said it was the hardest year of her life, and she still couldn't say if she had really made a good decision.

Every case is different. When living with an NP begins to suffocate you or harm your children, when the NP is so controlling that any separate thought or behavior in you sets off a tirade, or when you feel put down, fearful, or cut off from your family, friends, or the outside world, leaving may be the only way to have a calm emotionally secure life of your own, as in this example:

> Sarah's husband, Dan, had been in the military for most of their marriage. As he moved up the ranks in the intelligence division, she noticed that he was becoming more and more paranoid as well as demanding of her and especially their oldest son, Jake. Dan would shout and demand that dinner be at a certain time and that their two sons make all A's in school, and he expected to make every decision about the most mundane things.
>
> When their oldest son, Jake, was a junior in high school, he and his dad got into an all-out physical fight. The police were called, but Dan talked to them in his most charming way, and nothing came of it. However, their son Jake decided to move out and live with Sarah's mom and dad for his senior year. Sarah made sure that she sent money for Jake, but when Dan found out, he cut off all the money from Sarah.
>
> The younger son, Henry, and Sarah got jobs and stayed away from the house as much as they could. One night after Dan got into an argument with both

Sarah and Henry, Dan brought a gun into the house and put it in the bedside table. He said it was to protect them from their sons because he thought they might take revenge on him while he slept.

The next day, Sarah and the younger son moved out, and she filed for divorce. Sarah left everything behind so as not to create a court battle. She and the two boys stayed with her parents until the boys graduated from high school. Sarah said that if she hadn't had the support of her parents, she didn't know what she would have done.

NPs tend to adore you until they hate you. Often there is no in between. As long as things go the way the NP prefers, then the NP is happy and often generous and can even be boastful about his or her spouse and children but can be very quick to demand that his or her desires and wants be attended to at the expense of everyone else's.

Leaving a relationship with a highly intense NP can be challenging. The NP is likely to fight losing anything, such as possessions, money, children, community, prestige, and so on. It is usually the highly dysfunctional NP who will fight over custody of the children with the primary goal of not having to pay child support, who will hide family assets to keep from dividing property, and who will send harassing e-mails and texts demanding more and more time, energy, money, and attention.

If you need to take legal action to leave the NP, be sure to carefully interview prospective lawyers for their experience and approach for dealing with an antagonistic NP. Even if the NP in your life has not been hostile in the past, the prospect of losing money and attention can trigger strong possessive and hostile responses from the NP. You should be prepared to give up everything that isn't highly important to you and to fight for those things that are. Mediation with an NP is extremely unproductive and costly because the NP does not comprehend the concept of "fair."

It is important for anyone in a relationship with an NP to keep connected with family and friends for support, and it is always wise to have some money of your own, whether for things you need, for things you want for the children, or for leaving the relationship if things get intolerable.

BORDERLINE RELATIONSHIPS

Staying with the Borderline

Even under the best circumstances, the BP is very hard to live with. The BP's thoughts, feelings, delusions, and emotions and even his or her commitment to the relationship can shift so radically and so often that it keeps everyone on edge. The BP may have rages, jealousies, inconsistencies, and demands that can be impossibly difficult to deal with. It is also extremely difficult not to fall into the Caretaker role with the BP even when you are aware of the pattern and trying very hard to avoid caretaking.

If you stay with the BP, you will need to develop your own social life with your own friends in the community and at work, without the BP. BPs aren't comfortable in many social situations and typically prefer being at home or at very structured events where he or she knows everyone and is not expected to interact, such as going to a play or musical event. Here's a case of a former client who solved his dilemma.

> Martin married his high school sweetheart, Melissa. She was only 18, and he was 24. They had two children. Martin went to college and had a good career. When their daughters were five and seven years old, they moved away from Kansas City, where he and Melissa had grown up. This was the first time that Melissa had ever been away from her mother. Martin had known there were tensions and regular verbal arguments between Melissa and her mother, but he knew they were emotionally close. He didn't realize how unsettling the move would be for Melissa.
>
> After the move, Martin was astonished to find Melissa depressed, and then he saw that she was setting up ways to fight with him the same way she did with her mother. After 10 years, Martin was exhausted by Melissa's explosive anger and the bouts of depression she had after the anger subsided. She would be in bed for days. Her demands for him to stay home from work with her during the day and the equally strong demands for him to leave her alone became more than he could tolerate. She would be sweet and loving one minute and act like she hated him an hour later. Martin went to counseling with Melissa, and they were told that Melissa had borderline personality disorder. She was put on medication that made her moods less volatile, but her depression never really got better.
>
> When the children graduated from high school, Martin decided that he deserved to have a life of his own. However, he knew Melissa had only a high school education, few good social skills, and no way to really make a living on her own. As a Catholic, he also took his vows to his wife seriously. Melissa always had wanted to go back to Kansas City to be close to her mother. So Martin sold their 3,500-square-foot house and bought a condo in Kansas City for Melissa and a smaller home for himself and the girls in the town where they were going to college. Martin visited Melissa in Kansas City three or four times a year, and Melissa visited Martin and the girls several times a year. Martin felt that this way he was fulfilling his responsibilities to Melissa and his daughters and that he was finally feeling free to enjoy his life quietly doing the things he liked to do.

If you decide you want to stay with the BP in your life, do so with the full knowledge of what you are choosing to do. It does not seem loving or considerate to stay with the BP in order to change him or her, because you promised, or for the sake of the children. These are all really reasons that help you avoid feeling guilty. They are Caretaker reasons. Think through your reasons carefully because if you really are avoiding your own feelings of guilt and subconsciously hate and blame the BP for making your life miserable, you are dooming everyone in the family to misery with your decision to stay.

It may take some creativity to make life healthy and comfortable for you and the BP. Be open to alternative arrangements, such as Martin's. There are no hard-and-fast rules about how to live your life with the BP. Consider both of your needs and the needs of your children in making the arrangements that work best.

If you feel you are a person who can maintain your own sense of self, if you love and feel compassion for the BP, and if you are willing to voluntarily care for the BP without demanding that the BP change for you, then you could find a positive life with your BP spouse. Statistically, it is clear that very few people have all these qualities or can maintain them for decades at a time. Be sure you have a plan to get your own emotional and relationship needs met because the BP can't be counted on to provide you with the support, caring, and attention that you need for good mental health.

Leaving the Borderline

Because being in a relationship with a BP means being totally devoted to their care and needs, it is common for people to choose to leave the BP. The ups and downs of the BP's emotions as well as his or her tendency to blame loved ones for causing most of his or her pain is exhausting, and it is extremely difficult to keep your sanity and any sense of good feelings around the BP. BPs are often described as a "black hole" sucking up all the energy around them and rarely giving any of that energy back.

Despite knowing these emotional events will take place over and over again, you may still find it very hard to leave the BP. You may find it hard to quit feeling guilt or confusion around the BP. The BP hates you when you're there and loves you when you're gone.

Hoping that the BP will eventually be able to change leads only to greater and greater disappointment and frustration. I have often heard, "If only she could act this nice all the time" or "I know he is a really good person on the inside." Disappointment comes from your inability to keep all the conflicting parts of the BP in mind all of the time. Because you know that the BP is not very capable of caring for him- or herself, you may feel a great deal of guilt for leaving. Much of that guilt comes from your old Caretaker belief that it is your lifelong job to take care of the BP.

When you entered the relationship originally, you had the expectation that both of you were equally mentally and emotionally mature enough to take care of each other. When you confronted the fact that your partner had borderline personality disorder and became the Caretaker, you were trying to salvage the relationship. Now the question is whether you want to continue lifelong care for a mentally ill person.

Letting go of the relationship with the BP without malice and without guilt will help you leave without continuing your Caretaker patterns in future relationships. You may always find that you have a lot of caring to do for the BP even after a divorce, especially if you have children. Helping the children understand the illness of the BP parent and modeling for them functional interactions will be important to their mental health and development. You may have to supervise visits or plan them carefully so that the children and the BP can have as positive an experience as they can. This will benefit everyone.

On the other hand, if you do not have children, it is likely and maybe even preferable for both of you to sever the relationship completely. If you are clear that you do not want to be in the Caretaker role at all, then there is little benefit for you or the BP for the two of you to continue contact. Interactions with the BP are so difficult that neither of you is likely to find it enjoyable.

CHOOSING SEPARATION

Many Caretakers think that a separation will be a good way to ease out of the relationship with the BP/NP or to work on it from a distance. But check in with yourself to see if you may secretly be holding onto the hope that the separation might finally cause a change in the BP/NP. Separating as a means to force a change in the BP/NP is a Caretaker behavior and doomed to failure. As mentioned earlier, BP/NPs do not deal well with fuzzy boundaries. They see everything in black and white, and they need very clear boundaries to function well.

Separation creates a fuzzy, gray area that can be interpreted many different ways. So separation really is a situation where the BP/NP will be highly anxious because of the uncertainty of the relationship. For their own sense of security, the narcissist will generally choose to see a separation either as abandonment or as still being married. Borderlines, of course, tend to feel abandoned but still feel emotionally dependent.

In addition, you can't do positive work on a relationship with a mentally ill person without a clear commitment. Clearly severing the relationship makes the situation easier on everyone. The BP/NP needs a clear "yes" or "no," not a "maybe." If you feel strongly enough that the relationship is not working and you want to live apart, then you need to face that fact and make a decision, not put it off indefinitely by calling it a separation.

If you do end up deciding on a state of separation, set up clear rules and boundaries. Where will each of you live? Who will be paying for the rent, bills, groceries, and so on? If you have children, where will they be, and when will they be there? Will you have keys to each other's homes? What rules will you have about being in each other's space? You will actually have to make all the decisions you would need to make if you got a legal divorce in order to make a separation work.

LIMITED CONTACT VERSUS NO CONTACT

If you decide to end the relationship with the BP/NP, it is likely that the BP/NP will continue to initiate contact with you. If you have children together, it may be necessary for you to have some kind of contact with the BP/NP. It will be important for you to think through the frequency and kind of contact that will be comfortable and healthy for you.

Limited Contact

If you feel that you want or need to have at least some contact with the BP/NP, decide how much and when you want that contact based on your ability to interact with him or her in a civil, positive way. There are probably situations that you already know work better than others. It is important for you to take responsibility for making arrangements that work for you.

You definitely want to avoid any hysterics and hostility. There needs to be a good reason and purpose for having contact, usually due to legal interactions or child care arrangements. The BP/NP's preferred pattern is to always make you the Caretaker, so watch out about getting into situations where you are accommodating the BP/NP's needs but not your own.

Solutions for limited contact could include arrangements such as the following:

E-mail rather than face-to-face or phone contact
Online calendar sharing for child visitation
Drop-offs and pickups of children without entering each other's home
Meeting in public places
Taking a friend along when you meet with the BP/NP
Interacting only as long as both of you can be cordial
Leaving immediately if the BP/NP acts inappropriately
Not responding to texts or e-mails that are provocative
Limiting your conversation to essential information, preferably written
Using a third party to communicate
Getting all agreements in writing and sticking to them

Avoid participating in any crazy behavior. If you're on the phone with the BP/NP and he or she starts on a tirade, simply state, "If you are going to continue talking like that, I will hang up." Then do it. If you are in a face-to-face interaction, make the same statement and then leave if necessary. Do not engage in any discussion, reasoning, defending, and so on. It never works.

No Contact

If the BP/NP continues to perpetrate harm and hostility in the present, then eliminating direct contact may be the best option. A BP/NP who continues to blame you while justifying his or her own bad actions or who continues to create havoc and chaos in your life may never be emotionally safe. One of the hardest decisions that you may find you need to make is to severely limit or end contact with a harmful BP/NP.

Having no contact with the BP/NP may not end the pain, sadness, and anger that have resulted from that relationship, but it can be helpful in avoiding further negative interactions. Cutting off from the BP/NP is most beneficial when there is current, ongoing harm being done by the BP/NP or when just seeing or talking to him or her creates an intense emotional pain in you. Sometimes the effect of time and your own healing can make interactions more possible in the future. Unfortunately, in some situations, never seeing the BP/NP again is the only sane option.

If you decide on no contact, really follow through. No contact includes the following:

Not replying to e-mails, texts, or phone calls
Not sending cards, letters, or gifts
Using a third party (lawyer, accountant, or parenting coordinator) only to exchange necessary information
Not driving by or arranging to accidentally run into the BP/NP
Not following the BP/NP through social media

Also, keep your thoughts and actions aimed at making your own life happier and more enjoyable and stop spending time thinking, wondering, or worrying about the BP/NP.

TRYING TO BE FRIENDS AFTER LEAVING

It has become quite popular to offer to be "friends" with your ex-partner. Being friends after leaving is seen by some as being mature and the right thing to do. However, the BP/NP is not emotionally mature. That immaturity is what tugs at your nurturing, caretaking instincts. If you have left the relationship, the BP/NP will probably see you as disloyal, mean, traitorous, unfaithful, and abandoning. To offer to be friends at that point is insulting and feels like trickery to the BP/NP. It can also create fuzzy boundaries that can be misinterpreted. Basically, friendship with the BP/NP after the relationship ends is not likely and, again, must be entirely on the BP/NP's terms, so think through what you really want and be cautious.

SUMMARY

Whether you stay or leave or have little contact or no contact with the BP/ NP, remember that *it is your choice*. If you choose to stay with the BP/NP, you have a responsibility to do it with caring and love. Get support for yourself and learn to work with the BP/NP in positive ways. Talk to family members and friends for support and get into therapy to help you deal more effectively with the BP/NP while staying out of the Caretaker role.

If you choose to leave the relationship or have only limited contact, think it through to make it more workable. Remember that you have power only over what you do and say and not over what the BP/NP does. And if you decide to end contact with the BP/NP entirely, take on the responsibility for that choice and follow through.

III

Rebuilding

INTRODUCTION: HOW DOES IT LOOK TO NOT BE A CARETAKER?

Not being a Caretaker may seem hard to imagine, especially if you grew up being a Caretaker to a parent. It may seem strange to you at first when you start using the techniques outlined in this book. Breaking rules that you have used for many years and facing the fears you have about the possible repercussions can feel enormously uncomfortable and cause tremendous anxiety at first. Getting your mind changed from the rescuer, persecutor, and victim of the Drama Triangle to the actions of assertion, choice, and self-responsibility can take some time and some real concentration.

There are a lot of behaviors and attitudes that you will have to change in yourself as you move out of the Caretaker role. In this rebuilding phase, it will be very important to establish a network of support people, including family members, friends, and a therapist or support group, to help you move forward. These people can be your sounding board, giving you more objective feedback about who you are and what your abilities and skills are and reflecting and validating your personal qualities and traits. They need to be carefully chosen for their ability to see reality, their willingness to give you their time and attention, and their insight and understanding of the crazy-making relationship in which you are involved.

Carefully think through the steps of overcoming the Caretaker role that are outlined here and assess where you see yourself. This will help you to validate the skills and actions that you have already taken and help you identify what you still need to learn and practice. The new you is actually the *real* you. When you aren't caretaking another person's life, you are free to be who you really are, to reach out toward your potential, and to make a genuine contribution to your own life and to the lives of others.

Chapter Eighteen

Moving Forward in a Healthy Way

Whether you have a family member who is BP/NP or have had one or more relationships with BP/NPs, you do not have to be defined by those relationships. You have the power to make your interactions with the BP/NP more functional and productive by changing what you do, how you think, and what you believe about yourself and the BP/NP. These changes can make your life much more enjoyable, happier, and healthier. By pulling yourself and your interactions out of the Drama Triangle and moving into the Caring Triangle, you are also setting an example for others around you to improve their interactions with the BP/NP. You can stop giving your life energy away with no discernible results and instead make good use of that energy in your life and the lives of people around you.

THE CARING TRIANGLE

Caretakers work from the Drama Triangle of victim/persecutor/rescuer. Moving away from that drama to the Caring Triangle is the template for being a non-Caretaker. Instead of being a victim, you embrace acceptance and self-responsibility. Instead of persecuting, you become assertive and take action by doing. Instead of being a rescuer, you start making choices about your caring, as shown in the diagram in Figure 18.1.

CARING TRIANGLE

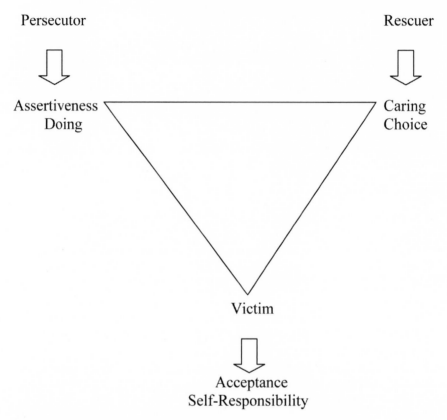

Figure 18.1.   The Caring Triangle with All Sides Working Together

By being assertive and doing, you take action without persecuting. You decide what you want and need, clearly state your goals and desires, and then take action to make those things happen in your life while still considering the feelings and needs of others. You don't ignore or invalidate anyone else's wants and needs, but you don't feel obligated to take care of those wants and needs for anyone else. By choosing with whom and how you want to be caring of others, you let go of being a rescuer and put your energies and efforts to good use in a way that you feel good about. Finally, and most important, you accept the facts of the mental illness of the BP/NP and accept self-responsibility for dealing with the BP/NP in the ways that you find healthy and rewarding rather than feeling resentful and manipulated.

One of the members of the Caretaker's recovery group put up a sign on her bathroom mirror: "No More Drama." This was her reminder every morning and evening to stay out of playing into the victim/persecutor/rescuer drama. It helped her to keep her emotions under control and step back from engaging in defensive, angry, tearful interactions with the BP/NP. She would look at the sign whenever she had to interact with the BP/NP as a reminder to think and choose her responses from an assertive, caring, and self-responsible place. Staying in the Caring Triangle is the best way to move toward a healthy life that is free from the Caretaker role.

DEALING WITH FEAR, OBLIGATION, AND GUILT RELAPSES

As you become healthier, keep on the lookout for the feelings of fear, obligation, and guilt to pop up when you are interacting with the BP/NP and don't be surprised if you get caught by one or more of them occasionally even after you feel you are well out of the Caretaker role. Fear, obligation, and guilt will continue to be the BP/NP's favorite tools for pulling you back into the Drama Triangle. Whenever you begin to have one of these feelings, check out consciously what is happening around you, step back, assess what triggered the feeling, and then take action to move out of that feeling before you find yourself pulled back into the drama. Stop your interaction with the BP/NP, if you can, until you get back on solid emotional footing.

Relapses are normal, and the less upset you get at yourself about them, the faster you can leave them behind. Go back to the positive self-talk techniques that helped you before and be sure that you don't go into self-blaming and negative self-criticism.

FEELING STRANGE IN A STRANGE LAND

It's not easy changing these patterns. Leaving the Caretaker role is a significant change in how you think and act and maybe how you feel. The way you feel about yourself, others, and even the whole of human interactions might be different. This takes some getting used to. And for awhile, it may take a good deal of vigilance. Old ways of doing things can feel so natural and can be done without thinking, while the new ways take attention and determination. Eventually, however, these new ways will become second nature to you. In the meantime, you may find that it is easier being yourself around people you have just met than with family members or old friends who can pull you into the old Caretaker patterns.

"I feel like I'm living in a different country with different ways of doing things," said David from the Caretaker's recovery group. He was reveling in doing many new things for himself that he had never done before and enjoying people being friendly and encouraging. He also said that sometimes he felt very unsure how to handle new situations or how to react to someone being so positive toward him. He couldn't always tell if the other person was sincere or putting him on. He just wasn't used to being treated in such a positive way. Sometimes he said he felt so happy and didn't know what to do with the increased energy he had. It was just like he was a different person, a stranger to himself.

As you recover from the Caretaker role, you may occasionally need to take time to retreat into your old feelings and compare them with the new feelings. Or you might be afraid that you could be hooked back into the old feelings and want to avoid anything that could take you back. Other times, you may find yourself feeling off kilter emotionally, mentally, or even physically. Alexia reported that when her NP mother died, she had waves of feeling physically dizzy and disoriented for several weeks. She decided it was related to the years she had spent emotionally "pushing" against her mother's invasive, controlling behaviors. Now that she didn't have to defend against that energy from her mother, she literally felt off balance for awhile.

You may find yourself wondering if you are "normal" in your responses or reactions to situations or people. Am I feeling too much or too little? Are my responses too friendly or too distant? Should I say something? What should I say? Having lived in a world where everything you said and did was criticized or judged as wrong by the BP/NP, you may find yourself feeling unsure what to say and do or even how to feel without that constant negative reflection. But that was more like the reflection from a circus fun house mirror, distorted and extreme.

What you really need now is your own inner awareness of who you are and what you want and need. Trust your own intuition in assessing situations and think about how you would want others to respond to you and do the same for them. In truth, most Caretakers have extremely good intuition. You have had to read the erratic ups and downs of the BP/NP for years, so it is likely that you can easily tune in to the interpersonal nuances in relationships. What tends to hold Caretakers in limbo is the fear of "doing the wrong thing," which really translates into doing something the NP/BP didn't like. Without the BP/NP there to criticize you, learn to trust your own reading of social situations and see how that works. It usually works very well. This means taking a chance on your own abilities to be normal. It can be a bit scary, but taking that chance and being successful can be very empowering.

KEEPING YOUR BOUNDARIES PROTECTED LONG TERM

As you get healthier and choose to live a happier, calmer, and less drama-oriented life, the BP/NP in your life will not be impressed. At first, the BP/

NP will try to reengage you by attacking or belittling you, making hurtful comments, observations, or judgments. When you do not reengage with the BP/NP in the old way of defending yourself, he or she will typically be at a loss as to how to interact with you.

If you quit playing the BP/NP/Caretaker game, the BP/NP is likely to increase his or her negative challenges for awhile. Eventually, if you continue to avoid responding to these provocations and, instead, avoid or take control of the interactions with the BP/NP, things will calm down. If you have cut off contact with the BP/NP, you may also see an increase in the BP/NP's trying to engage you, usually in a very negative way. The BP/NP can be very persistent, so you have to be just as persistent in continuing your new behaviors.

If you are still in relationship with the BP/NP, there may be less for you and the BP/NP to talk about or find to do together when you don't play by the rules of the game. Doing activities together that don't require verbal interaction often work the best. For example, going to the mall, going to a movie, watching television, hiking, bike riding, or attending a sports event usually work pretty well. Avoid long rides in a car, sitting around the house together, discussions about anything involving opinions or beliefs, or trying to work on a project together. These probably will not turn out well.

You may need to continually remind yourself that the BP/NP has little or no interest in what you think, what you are doing, what you want, and so on. If you want a friend—someone to listen and really understand what you're going through—look for an emotionally healthy person for that. Let the BP/NP talk about his or her own interests, and when you get bored, excuse yourself and leave.

You will now be in a more cordial relationship with the BP/NP, but it has limited content and pretty much no emotional connection. You may find yourself yearning for the few early days, weeks, or months of your relationship with the BP/NP when things were fun with the BP/NP and maybe even fabulous. These times will never come again, or they will be fleeting, perhaps because of a vacation, a tragedy, or some other loss that takes the BP/NP out of his or her ordinary level of functioning or away from his or her fear of needing you.

The important thing to remember is that you need to stay steadfast with your boundaries, keep your interactions with the BP/NP short and positive, and keep your own counsel about your choices of how you interact with the BP/NP. The BP/NP may attack you, or he or she may try to lure you back into the old relationship by being especially nice. Remember that the BP/NP wants you when you're gone but doesn't want you when you are there, and when you no longer fulfill any of his or her needs, you simply may cease to exist in his or her awareness.

WHEN THE BP/NP IS A FAMILY MEMBER

As you get control of your interactions with the BP/NP you have chosen to be with, remember to take a look at the BP/NPs who may be in your family of origin, such as parents, grandparents, or siblings. You can definitely use all the techniques covered in this book to improve those interactions as well. You can't easily cut off from a family member, so developing a new pattern with your family BP/NP will pay off in lifetime dividends. However, setting limits with a close family BP/NP may create a big distance between you because you are not playing the BP/NP/Caretaker game. Setting limits with the BP/NP can save you a lot of frustration and wasted anger while providing you and the BP/NP some positive interactions, as many examples in this book show.

Stepping out of your Caretaker role benefits you, the BP/NP, and the whole family. At first, you may get some emotional criticism from other family members for no longer being the Caretaker. When you are no longer caretaking, the BP/NP will work hard to increase his or her needs for caretaking with other family members. Over time, you may notice that the BP/NP does not actually need you, and you are setting a good model for others to follow to make their relationships with the BP/NP better as well. When you no longer interact frequently with the BP/NP because you have moved away, have your own family, or simply cut down on your contact, the BP/NP may quit thinking of you entirely.

> Nicholas had put a lot of energy and care into getting over being a Caretaker to his NP father. He reported that when his father was in the hospital at the end of his life and the family was gathered around, his father introduced everyone in the family, including Nicholas's two daughters, to the attending physician but omitted Nick. Nick was hurt at being omitted, but he also saw that as confirmation that his father no longer saw him as an extension of himself.

Being ignored or ceasing to exist to a BP/NP often isn't pleasant, but it does indicate that you are no longer their Caretaker. Keep in mind that *you*, as the unique individual who you are, may never have really existed for the BP/NP anyway. The BP/NP knows you are alive, but your individual feelings, values, interests, and ways of looking at the world have never existed in the BP/NP's conscious awareness.

If the BP/NP has the power and decides to actually kick you out of the family, feel assured that the BP/NP will make quite a production of telling you and everyone else that is the case. Caretakers can feel "orphaned" when this happens, especially if the BP/NP is a parent. You may feel resentful about being ignored or disregarded, or it may trigger you to beg to go back to being the Caretaker. Keep in mind that when you were playing into the drama of the BP/NP, you didn't like that even more.

At other times, the BP/NP may put you and your former relationship with him or her on a pedestal. The BP/NP may tell you how wonderful you used to be before you "pulled away," even though your memories of those experiences were of the BP/NP attacking and chastising you for everything. Or another family member may idealize the relationship you used to have with the BP/NP. After Kelly cut off contact with her BP sister as an adult, Kelly's mother continually tried to "get them back together," and Kelly had to hear over and over how sad and upset her mother was about the disconnection. This can feel very strange. And you can feel guilty for setting your own boundaries. Trying to please a family member who is still being a Caretaker may be impossible.

You need to decide not only how much to be around the BP/NP but also how much to be around the people who are still dancing to the BP/NP's game of victim/persecutor/rescuer. These may include parents, family friends, or maybe even your children. Anyone who is in a long-term relationship with the BP/NP may become upset when you quit the game of giving in to the BP/NP because then the BP/NP starts demanding more from them. When you quit the game, you shed light on the fact that they are still in the drama. In addition, they may become resentful that you don't have to "deal with" the BP/NP but that they still do. So it may actually be other family members, as well as the BP/NP, who are trying to draw you back into your old Caretaker role. Large family discussions, family social events, and emotionally difficult times can all be the setting for you to be pressured into resuming your Caretaker duties.

On the other hand, when you choose to deal with the BP/NP in ways that are less hurtful and damaging, this can also show everyone else that there are options for how to interact with the BP/NP. This can provide a model and give hope to other family Caretakers and give them permission to also re-think their Caretaker role.

Ultimately, you need to know yourself well enough to make the choices that work for you in relation to how, when, and where to spend time with the BP/NP in your family. Don't let the nagging, scolding, or pestering of the BP/NP and other Caretakers be the deciding factors. *You* have the right to be in charge of how you feel and act, so don't let the manipulations or pressures from other family members be your guide.

DECIDING TO LIVE YOUR OWN LIFE

The most common complaints that ex-Caretakers hear from the BP/NP are that you are being selfish, ungrateful, and wrong. Deciding to live your own life will probably be considered a betrayal to the BP/NP. To the BP/NP, the only choice is always the choice that he or she makes. So living your own life with your own values, goals, patterns, preferences, and so on will be considered wrong and disloyal to the BP/NP (and perhaps also to some of the other Caretakers around).

If you get only one life to live, why would you choose to live someone else's dream rather than your own? Your life is yours, and it is the only one you will get, so living your own dream and your own life in your own way seems to be the most logical and sensible choice to make. This does *not* mean you have to be uncaring or rejecting of anyone else's life choices. It is *not* selfish to choose a good life for yourself. It is *not* ungrateful to have different thoughts, needs, wants, or feelings from the BP/NP. You are *not* being disloyal by choosing differently. These accusations are the BP/NP's way of trying to control you to make him- or herself feel safer or more secure. You have the right and the responsibility to choose what and how much you do for others, and it is important to think long and hard before giving up on your own well-being for the transitory feelings of someone else.

CREATING

Living your own life, choosing for yourself, and being responsible for yourself instead of being focused on blaming the BP/NP allows you to bring into your life more of what you want. You are freer to think in new ways, try out new relationships, and observe accurately the results of what you actually do in your interactions with other healthy people. Many ex-Caretakers create a new sense of family that includes friends, healthy relatives, mentors, counselors, and other wise people. Find people to be close to who can help you create a healthy life for yourself and your loved ones.

BP/NP-dominated families tend to pass on beliefs such as: only blood relatives can be trusted, everybody in the family always agrees, never share anything personal with "outsiders," don't ask anyone for anything, and don't expect outsiders to be nice to you. It is a very fear-based worldview, and it is designed to be isolating, protected, and controlled by the BP/NP.

But there are many ways to create a close, caring relationship network. Think about your own deeply held values and beliefs. Create the image of a life that you think you would like and give it a try. Find others who practice more positive ways of communicating, be with those people more, and learn from them. Join in, ask, share, and create your own dream.

DOING WHAT YOU WANT WITH YOUR LIFE

From now on, it is all up to you to decide how you think, believe, feel, and act. As an ex-Caretaker, you know that it is your responsibility to do what you want with your life. This takes thought, deep consideration, and an ability to support yourself and your dreams. Making your own decisions about your life is what brings you peace and comfort and reduces the anxiety you used to feel. Owning your own life leads you to loving relationships, a satisfying career, solid friendships, and a sense of well-being within yourself. Keep moving to your own rhythm and in your own direction toward the life you want, and you will succeed.

Chapter Nineteen

Reaching Out to Others

To let go of the Caretaker role, you will need to reach out to others for friendship, caring, and support. This may be hard to do at first. As a Caretaker, it was important to preserve an image of perfection and family secrecy because these were important to the BP/NP. Really having close friendships and a support system were against the BP/NP's rules. However, emotional support, friendship, having fun, and enjoying your life are essential to being a normal, healthy adult rather than a Caretaker.

FINDING FRIENDS

As a Caretaker, you may have had very few close friends. Friends expect a reciprocal, fairly balanced interaction, which is different than you have been having with the BP/NP. Friends also expect you to follow through with the plans you make with them. After having to cancel numerous times to take care of an emotional meltdown by the BP/NP, friends tend to fall away and find people who are more available and reliable.

When you take steps to let go of the Caretaker role, friends are a very important part of your support system. They can be a sounding board, give you perspective, and help you figure out who you are and what you like to do. Look around and notice the people around you, such as those in a class, in a discussion group, at the grocery store, at the gym, and so on. Identify what you like about the people you observe. How are people like you? How are they different? What do you think you might enjoy doing with other people? What are the qualities you want in a friend?

Reach out to people who feel safe and comfortable to you. Try out a few simple activities, such as going for coffee or taking a walk. If you like the interaction, think of other things that you might be willing to do. Take these new interactions in slow chunks and let yourself notice how you feel, what you like, and what doesn't feel right, if anything.

In friendship, you are looking for give-and-take, back-and-forth. You do not want to get pulled into a Caretaker role with another BP/NP. Some things to consider in the early stages of a friendship to keep yourself out of the Caretaker role are the following:

Picking people with the qualities you value
Identifying the good qualities *and* the shortcomings of the person
Being aware of how much you each talk and share about yourselves
Observing how the two of you decide what to do and where to go
Observing whether this person has good boundaries without being too distant

Also, do a few things that you would never do as a Caretaker:

Ask the other person to do something that is inconvenient
Reschedule a get together
Identify something that you find uncomfortable about this new friend and let him or her know

Don't try to be perfect, don't be all-giving, don't just listen, and don't be too accepting. Instead, be as truly and honestly *you* as you can be. Try sharing some personal information, ask for help to do something, share everyday experiences, and keep your eyes and ears open for the qualities you want in a friend. Picking a friend is a very personal and self-fulfilling experience.

Each "friend" does not have to be your best friend forever. You may find one person you like to have lunch with, another for hiking, and another for supporting you as a parent. Take the good interactions and increase them and avoid the interactions that aren't as appealing. Build a variety of friendships at different levels. Some friends will be more emotionally close; others may not be. Some you may want to see a lot and others not as much. Spend time focused on positives, enjoy each other's competencies, and avoid using friendships for complaint sessions.

BUILDING RECIPROCITY

A real friendship is based on each person giving the other approximately the same amount of energy as each receives. Whether this energy is in the form of attention, invitations, gifts, advice, help, or understanding does not matter. This is called reciprocity and is the opposite of caretaking.

As a Caretaker, you were used to giving a lot more than you received, so you may think that non-Caretaker friendships are out of balance when you actually receive as much as you are giving. Other people need and want to give to you, so give them that chance. If you overgive, you will tend to make healthy people feel that you don't want or value what they can give to you, and you will tend to attract needy people who want a Caretaker. Having reciprocal friendships really helps you quit caretaking.

The exact form of giving and receiving doesn't really matter; rather, it is the *energy* that is exchanged. Notice how often each of you calls the other, who suggests the most activities, whether one person is paying for more things, who gives the most advice and help, who cancels the most, and so on. Work at keeping a balance by taking one step toward the other and waiting for the other person to take one step toward you. Especially watch the amount of energy each of you is giving. Does one person feel more needy of the other, does one person seem stronger, are either of you angry or hurt when the other doesn't call for awhile, or does either of you feel the relationship is "unfair" in any way?

If you feel the relationship is out of balance, don't demand that the less giving person give more. Notice the level of the energy exchanged and try matching the other person by giving more or giving less. See how that feels. Demanding that the other person give more or less or being hurt that the relationship is out of balance are old Caretaker feelings and behaviors.

HEALTHY PEOPLE CAN BE HONEST

Healthy relationships also include the ability to be honest and straightforward with each other. You can each ask for what you want, and you can each accept "no" as well as "yes" to simple requests without hostility or hurt feelings. Friends give each other reasons for their actions, requests, and responses. They "seek first to understand" the other. Defensiveness should be more of a rare response than the norm. When you have taken enough time to get to know someone, you should have built a level of trust and mutual acceptance that allows you to withhold judgment until you know the whole story. The two of you can problem solve together so that a mutually positive solution can be found. A good friendship also can become the model and provide the skills for a good love relationship.

HEALTHY FRIENDSHIP SKILLS

Having a healthy friendship includes the ability to share your thoughts and feelings, to describe your emotional processes, to not take what the other person says and does personally, and to trust that your friend will support and care about you even if he or she disagrees with you. Being a good friend takes a lot of sharing and caring back and forth.

When you find friends who give back to you, it can be very tempting to turn the tables and become the person who just receives. It can be heady and exciting and so fulfilling to be listened to, responded to, and cared about. But your friendships will no longer be true friendships if they begin to serve as ways to fill up your neediness left over from the past. If you notice a strong desire on your part to get more support and understanding from your friend than you are giving or more than the other person is comfortable with, that is a good time to call a professional therapist. A therapist can give you that extra attention, insight, and support in a way that is healthy. Keep caretaking out of your interactions (no matter which way it is going), and this will allow your budding friendship to mature and grow into a true sharing relationship.

HEALTHY FRIENDSHIP BOUNDARIES

Not being too invasive or too distant is important in keeping a friendship going. If the differences between the two of you are too great so that one person feels suffocated or one person feels ignored, then the boundaries are not mutually comfortable. Giving too much at once can feel invasive to one person, whereas never asking for consideration or understanding can end up feeling too distant. Set limits on any interactions that you find too uncomfortable but be open to new experiences.

Saying "no" is the most important boundary in any relationship. You have a right to disagree, to decline sharing too much personal information, to define how much time you are willing to give the friendship, or to set any other limits that you choose. Be respectful in setting these boundaries.

NOT ALL FRIENDSHIPS ARE FOREVER

Caretakers tend to believe that once you are friends with someone, you should never let the friendship go. As you move from being a Caretaker to being a whole and healthy person, you will inevitably find that some of your former relationships really don't meet the standards of being real friendships. Many of these friendships were actually a one-way giving of your energy to fix, help, rescue, or take care of someone; they were mutual complaint sessions about your relationships; or they just never were very fun, but that's all you thought you deserved.

As you learn to recognize and be comfortable with reciprocity, the worn-out, drained feeling you get from these old one-way relationships will become less and less attractive. However, as you give less and expect to be given to in a more equal way, you may notice these "friends" disappearing. Let them go. If you have to demand that the other person give an equal share of energy and attention, then the relationship has no real potential for health anyway.

Letting nonreciprocal relationships go without attack, rejection, criticism, or resentment is an art in itself. Keep in mind that *you* did a lot to maintain the imbalance in these relationships by accepting and putting up with the imbalance, by not asking for what you wanted, and/or by not leaving when the relationship didn't give you what you wanted. It is also likely that what you wanted in the past, such as being needed, being overly helpful, or being humble and undemanding, just aren't the things that you want in a friendship now. Be thankful for this former friend in teaching you to realize how an unbalanced relationship feels. Accept the lesson you have learned and let the person go with your blessing. He or she doesn't owe you anything since in the long run you may have learned more about being a healthy person than you ever could have without him or her.

LEARNING TO HAVE FUN

It really helps to have a friend or two (or more) with whom you can spend time just having fun. Fun is a necessary component of having a good, enjoyable, and healthy life. Look around you to find people who know how to have fun and who are also responsible. These people are good models, and you could try out some new fun things with them. Explore all kinds of fun things until you settle on the things that you really like. Classes, clubs, and groups focused around a certain activity can be a good way to start. By sharing an activity with a group, you will automatically make new friends who like to do the activity you are sharing.

Having friends who you have fun with will keep you motivated to let the Caretaker role go. You are more likely to follow through with a fun event if others are counting on you to be there. You could even make a weekly date with yourself to go out and do things you enjoy. Getting to know how you like to have fun is an essential part of knowing yourself, having an enjoyable life, and creating a life that is worth living.

OTHER WAYS OF REACHING OUT

Reaching out to others is the primary way we engage with the world. Isolation leads to feeling unvalued, unimportant, fearful, anxious, and depressed. The Caretaker role was very isolating. Rebuilding your sense of self means rejoining the world of other people, experiencing connections with others, and creating a life that you enjoy and that makes you feel truly good about yourself. Often clients ask me for ideas about how to do this. There are many ways to join *life*. Here are a few ideas:

For Self-Esteem

Get a professional portrait done.

Get a haircut, manicure, or pedicure.

Help people who really can appreciate your efforts, such as volunteering at a retirement home, school, or library.

Get a job that you really feel good about.

Make new friends and make time to be with them.

Accomplish something that you have wanted to do, such as publishing an article, painting a room, or washing your car.

Notice each time you do an activity how much you enjoy it or not.

Get rid of as many "have to and should" activities as possible.

Dress up once in awhile.

For Having Fun

Make a list of everything you have had fun doing in your lifetime and try some of them again.

Keep a journal of things you do each day and note how much fun each thing was.

Ask other people what they do for fun.

Read the weekly activities listed in the newspaper and pick out one to try.

Try a new restaurant once a month.

Go to an emotionally healing workshop every few months.

Take a class for fun and enjoyment, such as folk dancing, Japanese, culinary arts, watercolor, or photography.

For Your Health

Have a checkup once a year and actually go get the tests done.

Do something delightful for exercise, such as starting a garden, taking a hike, dancing, getting a dog and walking it, or learning to juggle.

Eat really well by selecting foods that are tasty and beautiful.

Take a deep, relaxing bath instead of a fast shower.

Read an inspiring book.

Learn to notice how your body feels.

Get really good sleep.

Get a massage or try yoga.

Life Direction

Everyday, ask yourself, "Am I living the life I choose?"

Look for happy surprises, such as spring buds or an unexpected compliment.

Notice how living your values enhances your life.

Take time to explore your own thoughts and feelings.

Notice who and what you appreciate in your life.

When you identify a problem, figure out how to solve it, then follow through.

If something is missing in your life, find a way to get it into your life, even if it takes awhile.

GETTING THERAPEUTIC SUPPORT

Earlier, I suggested that you find a knowledgeable therapist to help you come to a deeper understanding of the BP/NP and your role as Caretaker. In addition, a support group focusing on the issues that are specific to coping with Caretaker behaviors and letting them go is highly recommended. However, the group should focus specifically on letting go of caretaking and learning more effective coping behaviors with the BP/NP. The benefits of a Caretaker recovery group can be the following:

Learning that you are not alone in your experiences with the BP/NP.

Feeling understood and supported by others who really "get" what being a Caretaker is all about.

Getting ideas on ways to communicate more effectively with the BP/NP.

Having a safe place to get to know yourself, your likes and dislikes, and your feelings.

Creating a new image of how you want to live your life.

Learning skills to deal with your own emotional, thought, and behavioral distortions.

Learning to recognize when you are being a Caretaker and stopping the behaviors.

Developing a more positive sense of self.

Deciding on new relationship behaviors and getting support to follow through.

Taking steps for positive self-care.

Receiving encouragement.

Letting go of caretaking can create a healthier, happier life that is personally rewarding, but it takes attention, courage, insight, and practice. Having the support of others is essential. This is not a journey that can be done alone. You cannot let go of caretaking in isolation. You need others to provide feedback, insight, direction, encouragement, and support.

To truly let go of being a Caretaker and join other humans in enjoying life, you need to ask for and accept help and support, have good reliable friends, learn new relationship skills, find ways to have fun, revel in the beauty around you, experience activities that you love, and focus on being the real you; that is, create and develop your own real life. Only by really enjoying life can you make the truly unique and loving contribution that you have to make to the world.

Chapter Twenty

The New You

How do you see yourself without the Caretaker role? Do you have a clear picture? Are there some new behaviors that I have outlined that you find difficult to imagine? What old behaviors are a relief to let go? The following is a list of the behaviors and feelings that you release and let go of when you quit the Caretaker role and a list of skills, attitudes, and changes in your life that you gain.

Let Go Of:	**Gain:**
Victimization	Self-responsibility
Pleasing the BP/NP	Pleasing yourself
Trying to fix the BP/NP	Creating a life for yourself
Total responsibility	Self-responsibility
Rigid rules	Making healthy changes
Fear, obligation, and guilt	Assertion skills
Chronic self-sufficiency	Reaching out to others
Anger	Understanding
Tension and anxiety	Relaxed and clear
Powerlessness	Power over your own life
Focus on BP/NP	Focus on your own life
Hopelessness	Self-direction and life plan
Helplessness	Problem-solving skills

By working to let go of the debilitating and emotionally draining caretaking of the BP/NP, your life can be greatly improved. Work on creating a clear picture of yourself with all the attributes listed above. Making a visual image with a collage, a symbol, or a special phrase to represent who you are as a non-Caretaker can help you anchor these new insights, feelings, and beliefs; so you can instantly get in touch with your noncaretaker self by just bringing the image or phrase to mind.

BREAKING FREE OF YOUR CARETAKER IDENTITY

Becoming an ex-Caretaker takes determination, new skills, and persever-ance. Don't expect to get help, enthusiasm, or validation from the BP/NP for your efforts. However, you may find that the BP/NP is a lot more cooperative when you use the skills outlined in this book. The process of moving from being a Caretaker to becoming an emotionally healthy person usually takes some time, because it means changing long-term habits that control your emotional reactions, changing old thoughts and beliefs, and gaining a new understanding of the relationship between you and the BP/NP.

The process begins with your awareness of your own emotional, thought, behavioral, and relationship distortions that were described in earlier chap-ters. Letting go of your thinking and expectations that the BP/NP will "get well" or change helps you move through the process. Creating new thought patterns and relationship interactions that are based on the *reality* of the BP/NP's level of dysfunction can also help. Getting control of your emotional reactions and your ineffective responses to the crazy-making actions of the BP/NP will move you along. Ultimately, these changes lead you to see your-self and the BP/NP in different, more honest and realistic ways. You then have the tools to decide for yourself the kind of life you want to lead. The real change happens when you identify the boundaries and limits you need to set against the encroachment of the BP/NP into your life and begin putting those into place day by day. Reaching out, making new friends, and getting support from healthy people gives you the strength you need to finally let go of your dependence on "giving" as the basis of your self-esteem. By the time you have accomplished these things, you will have become a non-Caretaker.

STEPS IN OVERCOMING THE CARETAKER ROLE

Over the years, clients have asked me to give them an outline of the steps they need to take to stop caretaking. Here is what I give them:

Increase Your Self-Esteem

You have to feel good enough about yourself that you no longer are content treating yourself like a second-class citizen. You have to change your inner self-talk from negative and demeaning to positive, self-supportive, and self-encouraging. The skills outlined in this book that will help you increase your self-esteem, including treating yourself well both mentally and physically, assertion skills, setting boundaries, letting go of believing that you can fix the BP/NP, and creating and moving toward positive goals for your own life.

Take Care of Your Own Needs Yourself

Instead of expecting the BP/NP to meet your needs, take over the responsibility to meet your own needs through your own efforts. This means letting go of your *expectation* that the BP/NP *should* or *ought to* think of your needs before his or her own; or want to do what you want him or her to do; or problem solve for you; or plan, direct, or organize things that you want to do; or step in and take care of things when you are tired or ill. It means that you will make your own plans and take care of whatever you decide you want to have done. It does not mean that you can't *ask* the BP/NP to help with these things, but you have let go of your expectation that he or she must do these things for you.

Become Financially Independent

If you do not have some financial independence from the BP/NP, your options will be severely limited. This means that you need to have some income of your own or savings that the BP/NP cannot touch, and you need a car in your name. In addition, it is really helpful if you do not have any credit card debt. If you are married, it may be that both you and your BP/NP spouse are responsible for certain debts. Even though you may not be able to control the BP/NP's spending, you can control your own. When people are depressed or anxious, they sometimes buy things to calm those feelings. Really taking good care of yourself includes not putting yourself in debt for unnecessary things, so don't use "retail therapy" to try to make yourself feel better. It results in eliminating choices and options that could make your life more livable.

If you are a woman with young children and in a BP/NP relationship, you will have the least number of options for making your own decisions and taking care of yourself and the children if the BP/NP suddenly leaves or you find the relationship becoming intolerable. Being in a financially sound position allows you the time and space to take the actions that you choose rather than being forced into situations that you think are unhealthy or create a great deal of distress. So you will need to create a plan for making yourself more financially independent in order to increase your options.

Develop a Support Network

Throughout this book, I have emphasized that you need friends and family members who are emotionally supportive of you. In order to get that support, you will need to let them know at least some information about the relationship situation that you are in. You can't get the support you need if no one knows what is going on in your relationship. On the other hand, you don't want to make your friendships focused entirely on the dynamics of your interactions with the BP/NP. So having a therapist or therapy group will also be important to your getting out of the Caretaker role. You need people who will be objective and helpful in pointing out when you are falling back into Caretaker mode. And you need people to have fun with and remind you of who you are away from your relationship with the BP/NP. These friends, family, and professionals are the people who will support you and validate you and on whom you can rely in times of need. They are at the center of your sense of reality.

Stop Playing the BP/NP Games

Learning and using the communication model, being assertive, and figuring out creative ways to break the rules will be at the core of your switching yourself out of the Caretaker role. You cannot change anything in this relationship as long as you follow the BP/NP's rules. The BP/NP will not willingly give up playing by his or her own rules, so you will have to be the one to make changes. This takes a lot of courage, insight, and tenacity. It will require you to "toughen up" so that you will be less affected by the emotional reactions of the BP/NP. That is why increasing your self-esteem, becoming more emotionally and financially independent of the BP/NP, and developing a support system of people who love and care about you are essential.

Quit Trying to Change the BP/NP and Change Yourself

All of this adds up to your moving your focus from trying to change the BP/NP to changing yourself into being the person you want to be. You ultimately give up being the Caretaker when you give up your need to change the BP/NP. When you begin seeing caretaking as the thankless and impossible task that it is, you will find it easier to let it go. This is not a selfish move. It is an act of compassion, caring, understanding, and honesty to both you and the BP/NP to quit trying to change him or her.

Define and Create Your Own Life

This is ultimately the primary responsibility you have in life—that is, to be who you are, to be the best person doing the most of what is right for you.

When you define your own life, you become responsible for who and what you are, and you have the best chance to make your greatest contribution to your family, your friends, your work, and your community. You can let helplessness, hopelessness, resentment, exasperation, frustration, and bitterness all go. You do have power to make your life enjoyable, productive, and pleasurable when you make it your priority to do so.

BECOMING CONGRUENT INSIDE AND OUT

As a Caretaker, you lived a double life. Although you were competent, friendly, cooperative, and effective at work, at school, and in your friendships, at the same time, you were consumed by fear, obligation, guilt, passivity, powerlessness, and hopelessness as you interacted with the BP/NP. Letting go of the Caretaker role with the BP/NP gives you the chance to act more congruently by being who you really are and behaving in all relationships (even with the BP/NP) in ways that reflect your true, healthy, responsible, and hopeful sense of self.

You are no longer controlled by the BP/NP's emotional neediness and anxiety. You no longer pick up his or her fear, anger, alarm, and dismay. You can hold on to your own view of the world and your own feelings of hope, confidence, and trust in the goodness of yourself and others. You can have healthy friendships, joyful interactions with others, creative insights, and energy to follow through with things you really want to do in your own life. You can be more fully who *you* are.

OPEN THE DOOR TO YOUR NEW LIFE

Don't put off any longer moving toward your own healthy, productive life. Follow the steps that are outlined here and put your energy into doing those things. Every time you pull your energy away from the old, unproductive behavior patterns of being the Caretaker, you will have more energy to take these new steps. What will your life look like? Maybe it could look like this visualization.

> Imagine waking up in the morning rested and looking forward eagerly to the day to come—a day that is filled with work, friends, and fun that you have chosen, activities that fulfill you and give you pleasure and interactions that are supportive and validating. You find yourself looking with anticipation to the future. You are doing your fair share of the work in your life, you can count on getting help from others, and you can be at ease even when things don't work out perfectly. You feel free. You are free.
>
> The decisions in your life are the ones you have thought through and made because they feel right for you. You find yourself feeling and being successful

as you share who you are and your abilities with others. You receive appreciation and recognition from those in your life whom you have helped, and you feel deserving of their caring and positive regard.

You know that when you are tired and overwhelmed, you can count on these loving people to help and support you. They think of you and share their loving energy with you when you are down. They are there in your times of need. You feel fulfilled and content, and you are following your own life's plan. You are responsible for yourself, and you have much to offer to others. You have value. You have worth. You are complete.

Let yourself reflect on these images and thoughts. Let yourself truly feel how your life could be this way. Whatever you imagine clearly and wholeheartedly is what your subconscious mind will steer you toward. Keep your compass pointed toward your own truth and put your energy into reaching that truth.

So be it.

Appendix

Caretaker Test

Circle the number that most accurately reflects how you *act* in your significant relationship with a partner, coworker, or family member; 1 represents "almost never," and 5 represents "almost always."

1. I find it hard to say "no" to my partner.	1 2 3 4 5
2. I often do not know what I want.	1 2 3 4 5
3. I frequently find myself angry or upset after talking to my partner.	1 2 3 4 5
4. Even when I tell my partner "no," I find myself doing what he or she wants anyway.	1 2 3 4 5
5. I find that I have given up friendships to please my partner.	1 2 3 4 5
6. When my partner says mean or disparaging comments to me, I ignore them or hide my hurt.	1 2 3 4 5
7. I have learned to act "as if" I am okay even when I'm not.	1 2 3 4 5
8. I put up with a lot of behaviors from my partner that my friends would not.	1 2 3 4 5
9. I find that I have to say things very carefully to my partner, or he or she will get angry or hurt.	1 2 3 4 5
10. I cover up behaviors and comments that my partner makes that are rude or hurtful.	1 2 3 4 5
11. I expect myself to be more responsible than other people.	1 2 3 4 5
12. I should always try to make my partner feel better when he or she feels angry, hurt, or sad.	1 2 3 4 5
13. I often feel that people let me down.	1 2 3 4 5

14. I hold myself to more exacting standards than I hold my partner. 1 2 3 4 5

15. I know I could make my partner feel and act better if I would just do what he or she wants. 1 2 3 4 5

16. If my partner is happy, then I am happy. 1 2 3 4 5

17. When I have a desperate need to be close and connected with my partner, he or she rarely wants to. 1 2 3 4 5

18. I know that it is entirely up to me to make things work with my partner. 1 2 3 4 5

19. When things are going well with my partner, I can forget our problems. 1 2 3 4 5

20. I chastise myself for behaviors that I forgive and accept in others. 1 2 3 4 5

21. I can't be happy unless my partner is happy. 1 2 3 4 5

22. I can't seem to predict whether my partner will be happy or angry in any given situation. 1 2 3 4 5

23. I am convinced that if I just try hard enough, I can get my partner to be nicer to me. 1 2 3 4 5

24. I feel the most love toward my partner when I am not in his or her presence. 1 2 3 4 5

25. I find I am bored in relationships that do not have a lot of intensity or emotion. 1 2 3 4 5

26. I often feel confused or surprised by my partner's reactions to everyday problems. 1 2 3 4 5

27. It is more important to me to make my partner happy than to be happy myself. 1 2 3 4 5

28. Although I am often angry at my partner, I just try harder to please him or her. 1 2 3 4 5

29. Every time my partner is happy or pleased, I find my hope renewed that our relationship will now be much better. 1 2 3 4 5

30. Even when I feel hopeless about the relationship with my partner, I feel extremely guilty about leaving him or her. 1 2 3 4 5

31. Being rejected by my partner is the worst thing that I can think of happening to me. 1 2 3 4 5

32. When someone I don't know very well is being especially nice to me, I feel nervous or uncomfortable or undeserving. 1 2 3 4 5

33. I do nice things for my partner, and then I get angry when he or she doesn't do nice things for me.   1 2 3 4 5

34. I try to anticipate my partner's needs or wants so that he or she will be pleased with me and not be angry.   1 2 3 4 5

35. I feel depressed or discouraged, but I don't know why.   1 2 3 4 5

36. I feel extremely nervous or anxious around my partner.   1 2 3 4 5

37. The more perfect I can be, the better people like me.   1 2 3 4 5

38. I try to never make mistakes.   1 2 3 4 5

39. I find it hard to sit quietly for even a few minutes.   1 2 3 4 5

40. I find it hard to express anger outwardly, so I keep it to myself, although sometimes I finally blow up.   1 2 3 4 5

SCORING

1–80   **Non-Caretaker.** You have a sympathetic and kindhearted nature. You have some distortions in your thinking, but they don't get in your way.

81–120   **Protesting Colluder.** You may never have been a Caretaker in other relationships, but you find yourself feeling guilty and responsible for this partner. Your high level of loyalty and logic keep you determined to work on this relationship until you get it right.

121–160   **Pathological Altruism.** No matter how hard you try in this relationship, you often feel disappointed, depressed, and unappreciated. Although you would like to be treated better, you ignore or reject help, compliments, and kindness from others, preferring to do things yourself. You often feel depressed.

161–200   **Self-Defeater.** You have been in numerous relationships where you felt rejected, humiliated, or unloved. You may not even remember a time when you felt hopeful or happy. You may have been sexually or physically abused, and you don't feel deserving of love. Yet you have a determination to keep trying to make your relationships work, and you keep alive a wish to have love and caring in your life.

Notes

1. IS MY PARTNER REALLY A BORDERLINE OR NARCISSIST?

1. M. M. Linehan, *Cognitive-Behavioral Treatment of Borderline Personality Disorder* (New York: Guilford Press, 1993).
2. M. M. Linehan, *Cognitive-Behavioral Treatment of Borderline Personality Disorder* (New York: Guilford Press, 1993).
3. Robert O. Friedel, *Borderline Personality Disorder Demystified* (New York: Marlowe & Co., 2004), 67–74.
4. American Psychiatric Association, *Diagnostic and Statistical Manual of Mental Disorders*, 4th ed. (Washington, DC: American Psychiatric Association, 1994), 633, 650–54.
5. Friedel, *Borderline Personality Disorder Demystified*, 66–67.
6. S. Johnson, *Character Styles* (New York: Norton, 1994), 171.

2. WHY THE BORDERLINE/NARCISSISTNEEDS A CARETAKER

1. V. Satir, *The New Peoplemaking* (Palo Alto, CA: Science and Behavior Books, 1988).
2. V. Satir et al., *The Satir Model* (Palo Alto, CA: Science and Behavior Books, 1991).
3. Stephen Karpman, "The New Drama Triangles" (paper presented at USATAA/ITAA conference, August 11, 2007), available at www.KarpmanDramaTriangle.com.

3. WHAT IS A CARETAKER?

1. R. Kreger and J. P. Shirley, *Stop Walking on Eggshells Workbook* (Oakland, CA: New Harbinger, 2002),129–38.
2. Robert O. Friedel, *Borderline Personality Disorder Demystified* (New York: Marlowe & Company, 2004), 63–74.

4. CARETAKER INVOLVEMENT LEVELS

1. B. Oakley et al., eds., *Pathological Altruism* (New York: Oxford University Press, 2011).

9. RELATIONSHIP DISTORTIONS OF CARETAKERS

1. Gerald Corey, *Theory and Practice of Counseling and Psychotherapy*, 6th ed. (Belmont, CA: Brooks/Cole, 2001), 198–99.

13. INCREASING YOUR SELF-CONFIDENCE

1. *Merriam Webster's Collegiate Dictionary*, 11th ed. (Springfield, MA: Merriam Webster, 2003).

Bibliography

Bader, Ellyn, Peter Pearson, and Judith Schwartz. *Tell Me No Lies.* New York: Skylight Press, 2000.

Bateman, Anthony, and Peter Fonagy. *Psychotherapy for Borderline Personality Disorder: Mentalization-Based Treatment.* Oxford: Oxford University Press, 2004.

Beattie, Melodie. *Beyond Codependency and Getting Better All the Time.* New York: Harper & Row, 1989.

———. *Codependent No More: How to Stop Controlling Others and Start Caring for Yourself.* New York: Harper & Row, 1987.

Berry, Carmen R. *When Helping You Is Hurting Me: Escaping the Messiah Trap.* San Francisco: Harper, 1989.

Brach, Tara. *Radical Acceptance: Embracing Your Life with the Heart of a Buddha.* New York: Bantam Dell, 2003.

Brown, Eva M. *My Parent's Keeper: Adult Children of the Emotionally Disturbed.* Oakland, CA: New Harbinger, 1989.

Brown, Nina. *Children of the Self-Absorbed.* Oakland, CA: New Harbinger, 2001.

———. *Loving the Self-Absorbed.* Oakland, CA: New Harbinger, 2003.

Carter, Steven, and Julia Sokol. *Men Who Can't Love.* New York: Berkley, 1987.

Cohen, C., and V. R. Sherwood. *Becoming a Constant Object in Psychotherapy with the Borderline Patient.* Northvale, NJ: Jason Aronson, 2002.

Corey, Gerald. *Theory and Practice of Counseling and Psychotherapy.* 6th ed. Belmont, CA: Brooks/Cole, 2001.

Deroo, Carlene, and Carolyn Deroo. *What's Right with Me.* Oakland, CA: New Harbinger, 2006.

Donaldson-Pressman, Stephanie, and Robert M. Pressman. *The Narcissistic Family: Diagnosis and Treatment.* New York: Lexington, 1994.

Evans, Patricia. *Controlling People.* Avon, MA: Adams Media, 2002.

———. *The Verbally Abusive Relationship.* Holbrook, MA: Adams Media, 1996.

Farmer, Steven. *Adult Children of Abusive Parents.* New York: Ballantine, 1989.

Forward, Susan. *Toxic Parents.* New York: Bantam, 1989.

Foster, Rick, and Greg Hicks. *How We Choose to Be Happy.* New York: Berkley, 1999.

Freeman, Arthur, and Gina M. Fusco. *Borderline Personality Disorder: A Therapist's Guide to Taking Control.* New York: Norton, 2004.

Friedel, R. O. *Borderline Personality Disorder Demystified.* New York: Marlowe, 2004.

Fusco, Gina M., and Arthur Freeman. *Borderline Personality Disorder: A Patient's Guide to Taking Control.* New York: Norton, 2004.

Glickauf-Hughes, Cheryl, and Marolyn Wells. *Object Relations Psychotherapy.* Northvale, NJ: Jason Aronson 1997.

Hotchkiss, Sandy. *Why Is It Always about You?* New York: Free Press, 2003.

Johnson, Stephen M. *Character Styles.* New York: Norton, 1994.

———. *Humanizing the Narcissistic Style.* New York: Norton, 1987.

Karpman, Stephen. "The New Drama Triangles." Paper presented at USA Transactional Analysis Association/International Transactional Analysis Association Conference, August, 11, 2007.

Klatte, Bill C., and Kate Thompson. *It's So Hard to Love You: Staying Sane When Your Loved One Is Manipulative, Needy, Dishonest or Addicted.* Oakland, CA: New Harbinger, 2007.

Kreger, R., and James Shirley. *The Stop Walking on Eggshells Workbook.* Oakland, CA: New Harbinger, 2002.

Kreger, R., and K. Williams-Justesen. *Love and Loathing: Protecting Your Mental Health and Legal Rights When Your Partner Has Borderline Personality Disorder.* New York: Book Clearing House, 1999.

Kreisman, J., and Hal Straus. *I Hate You—Don't Leave Me: Understanding the Borderline Personality.* New York: Avon, 1991.

———. *Sometimes I Act Crazy.* Hoboken, NJ: Wiley, 2004.

Lawson, C. A. *Understanding the Borderline Mother.* Northvale, NJ: Jason Aronson, 2000.

Lerner, Harriet G. *The Dance of Anger.* New York: Harper & Row, 1985.

Linehan, Marsha M. *Cognitive-Behavioral Treatment of Borderline Personality Disorder.* New York: Guilford, 1993.

Manfield, Philip. *Split Self/Split Object.* Northvale, NJ: Jason Aronson, 1992.

Manning, Shari Y. *Loving Someone with Borderline Personality Disorder.* New York: Guilford, 2011.

Mason, P., and Randi Kreger. *Stop Walking on Eggshells.* Oakland, CA: New Harbinger, 1998.

Masterson, James F. *The Narcissistic and Borderline Disorders: An Integrated Developmental Approach.* New York: Brunner/Mazel, 1981.

———. *The Search for the Real Self: Unmasking the Personality Disorders of Our Age.* New York: Free Press, 1988.

McCormack, C. C. *Treating Borderline States in Marriage.* Northvale, NJ: Jason Aronson, 2000.

Meier, Paul, and Robert L. Wise. *Crazymakers.* Nashville: Thomas Nelson, 2003.

Miller, Alice. *The Body Never Lies.* New York: Norton, 2005.

Millon, Theodore, Seth Grossman, Carrie Millon, Sarah Meacher, and Rowena Ramnath. *Personality Disorders in Modern Life.* 2nd ed. Hoboken, NJ: Wiley, 2004.

Missildine, W. Hugh. *Your Inner Child of the Past.* New York: Simon & Schuster, 1963.

Morrison, Andrew P. *Shame: The Underside of Narcissism.* Hillsdale, NJ: Analytic Press, 1989.

Neuharth, Dan. *If You Had Controlling Parents: How to Make Peace with Your Past and Take Your Place in the World.* New York: Harper Collins, 1998.

Oakley, B., Ariel Knafo, Guruprasad Madhavan, and David S. Wilson, eds. *Pathological Altruism.* New York: Oxford University Press, 2011.

Ronningstam, Elsa F. *Identifying and Understanding the Narcissistic Personality.* New York: Oxford University Press, 2005.

Rosenberg, Marshall. *Nonviolent Communication: A Language of Life.* Encinitas, CA: Puddle Dancer Press, 2003.

Roth, Kimberlee, and Freda Friedman. *Surviving a Borderline Parent: How to Heal Your Childhood Wounds and Build Trust, Boundaries, and Self-Esteem.* Oakland, CA: New Harbinger, 2003

Satir, Virginia. *The New Peoplemaking.* Palo Alto, CA: Science & Behavior Books, 1998.

Satir, V., J. Banman, J. Gerber, and M. Gomori. *The Satir Model.* Palo Alto, CA: Science & Behavior Books, 1991.

Schore, A. N. *Affect Dysregulation and Disorders of the Self.* New York: Norton, 2003.

Sharff, J., and D. E. Sharff. *The Primer of Object Relations Therapy.* Northvale, NJ: Jason Aronson, 1995.

Siegel, D., and J. Young. *Disarming the Narcissist: Surviving and Thriving with the Self-Absorbed.* CA: New Harbinger

Thomas, Alexander, S. Chess, and A. Birch. *Behavior and Individuality in Early Childhood.* New York: New York University Press, 1964.

Tinman, Ozzie. *One Way Ticket to Kansas: Caring about Someone with Borderline Personality Disorder and Finding a Healthy You.* San Bernardino, CA: Bebes & Gregory Publications, 2005.

Index

About the Author

Margalis Fjelstad, PhD, LMFT, has a private psychotherapy practice in Ft. Collins, Colorado, specializing in work with clients who are in relationship to someone who has borderline or narcissistic personality disorder, and she facilitates groups on Caretaker recovery. She has previously been an Adjunct Faculty member at Regis University in Colorado Springs and at California State University in Sacramento.

Made in United States
North Haven, CT
02 May 2023

36164623R00138